Mission Santa Ines

SANTA INES, VIRGEN Y MARTIR

...aries of California

New Series. Local History

Mission Santa Ines

VIRGEN Y MARTIR

AND ITS

ECCLESIASTICAL SEMINARY

BY

Fr. ZEPHYRIN ENGELHARDT, O. F. M.

*Author of "The Missions and Missionaries," "The Franciscans
in Arizona," "Mission Dolores," "Mission San
Diego," "Mission Santa Barbara,"
"Mission San Gabriel," etc., etc.*

*"Colligite quae superaverunt fragmenta,
ne pereant," John, vi, 12.*

McNally & Loftin, Publishers

1986

Santa Barbara

Imprimi Potest,

FR. NOVATUS BENZING, O. F. M.,
Minister Provincialis

Nihil Obstat,

M. F. WINNE, C. M.,
Censor Deputatus

Imprimatur,

JOHN CAWLEY, Vicar General
July 14, 1932.

McNally & Loftin, Publishers
P.O. Box 1316
Santa Barbara, CA 93101

Printed at Kimberly Press, Inc.

Library of Congress Cataloging-in-Publication Data

Englehardt, Zephyrin, 1851-1934.
  Mission Santa Inés, Virgen y Mártir, and its ecclesiastical seminary.

  Reprint. Originally published: Santa Barbara, Calif: Mission Santa Barbara,
1932. (Missions and missionaries of California. New series, Local history)
  Includes bibliographical references and index.
  1. Santa Inés Mission (Solvang, Calif.)—History—Sources. 2. Solvang
(Calif.)—Church history—Sources.
I. Title.
F869.S68E54   1985   979.4′91   85-23977
ISBN 0-87461-063-X
ISBN 0-87461-062-1 (pbk.)

Reissue Preface

Friar Zephyrin Engelhardt (1851-1933) became the Dean of California Mission Historians based on his four volume *Mission and Missionaries of California,* published between 1908 and 1915. His position, however, was secured by a series of sixteen studies of individual missions published from 1920 to 1934.

Mission Santa Ines Virgen y Martir was originally published in 1932 and was long out of print. The current reissue is part of a program of research and historic preservation at Mission Santa Ines. Republication of *Mission Santa Ines Virgen y Martir* was funded by a grant from the Royal Scandanavian Inn, Solvang, California. Their support is gratefully acknowledged.

Thanks are due to Mr. Richard Whitehead and Ms. Julia Costello for their advice and assistance.

Pandora E. Snethkamp
Center for Archaeological Studies
University of California
Santa Barbara, California

PREFACE

Missions Santa Inés is one of the three Franciscan Missions, which are situated in Santa Barbara County. The manuscript, containing its local history, was completed nearly a decade ago. The lack of funds, however, caused the publication to be postponed until the present time.

A recent and serious illness of the author brought about more delay. In these adverse circumstances, Rev. Fr. Felix, O. F. M., cheerfully agreed to supervise the printing of the book and the arrangement of the illustrations in accord with the author's directions.

Grateful acknowledgment is hereby made to Mr. Edward Borein, of Santa Barbara, California, for the beautiful cover design; to Brother Gerard, O. F. M., for re-typing the copy; to Brother Matthew, O. F. M., for reading the proofs; to Brother Seraphin, O. F. M., for making a number of drawings.

THE AUTHOR.

CONTENTS

Contents

Page
CHAPTER XII.

CHAPTER XIII.

APPENDIX

Page

ILLUSTRATIONS

SECOND MILITARY DISTRICT
IV
SANTA INES MISSION
(1804-1850)

THE OLD
FRANCISCAN
MISSIONS
IN
CALIFORNIA.

Scale of Miles.

0   50   100   150

Rand, McNally & Co.

CHAPTER I.

Search for Mission Sites.—Report of Fr. Estévan Tápis.—Viceroy's Permit.—Governor Arrillaga.—Death of Fr. Presidente Lasuén.—Fr. Presidente Estévan Tápis.—Mission Founded.—First Baptisms.—Unnecessary Warning.

Ever since the indefatigable Franciscan explorer, Fr. Hermenegildo Francisco Garcés of Mission San Javier del Bac, Arizona, in 1776 penetrated to the interior of California, to the region of the Tulares, it was known that numerous Indian tribes occupied the country east of the sierras. The insatiable zeal of the missionaries longed to bring them into the fold of Christ; but several gaps in the mission chain along the coast still existed, and numerous rancherias within sight of the ocean had not as yet heard the saving truths of Christianity. No sooner had the superior of the Missions, Father Fermín de Lasuén, in 1797 filled the gaps by establishing the Missions of San José, San Juan Bautista, San Miguel, and San Fernando, and in 1798 the Mission of San Luis Rey, than he directed Father Estévan Tápis of Mission Santa Barbara to accompany Captain Felipe de Goycoechea and survey the region east of the sierras for suitable Mission sites. It was not safe nor practicable to plant a Mission so far away as the Tulare Valley. The missions now were situated only a day's journey from one another, and at this distance from the nearest Mission it was decided to found the next missionary center.

Fr. Tápis set out from Santa Barbara with the captain of the presidio and some guards on October 17, 1798. On the first day out they reached the rancheria of Tegueps. Here Fr. Tápis baptized an Indian woman who lay grievously ill in her shack. On the 18th, at 7 p. m., the expedition reached the rancheria of Calahuasa, the objective point, but the journey was continued to the rancheria of Alajulapu, which Fr. Lasuén had commissioned Fr. Tápis to examine closely. "I informed myself," Fr. Tápis reported, "about the number of rancherias nearer to said place (Alajulapu) than to either the Missions of Purisima or Santa Barbara. I discovered the following rancherias, and their distances from Alajulapu are added.

Calahuasa, thirty lodges, two and one-half leagues:
Jonata, sixteen lodges, three leagues:
Ahuaslayec, twenty huts, three leagues:
Tegueps, twenty-five lodges or huts, four leagues:
Sotonocmu, fifty huts, four leagues:
Aquitsumu, twenty huts, seven leagues:
Asnisehuc, twenty-five huts, nine leagues:
Sishuohuo, eight huts, nine leagues:
Stucu, twenty-five huts, nine leagues:
Huilioqui (Ituililic), eight cabins, nine leagues:
Ituenegil, fifty habitations, about twelve leagues:
Anajue, twenty habitations, three leagues:
Sauchu, or Santa Rosa, twelve huts, four leagues:
Elemana, ten habitations, five leagues.

Multiplying the 277 habitations in the first ten rancherias by four, the number of persons I count for each, the result will be 1,008 pagan Indians. This calculation appears to me to be correct, and in accordance with what I have experienced in the rancherias on the coast. Converts from these rancherias are generally baptized at Mission Purisima."[1]

On the strength of this report, which was communicated by Fr. Lasuén to Governor Diego Borica, the latter recommended the region of Calahuasa to the viceroy as a suitable locality for the new Mission. Meanwhile, José Joaquin de Arrillaga had succeeded Borica as governor of California. Under date of March 2, 1803, viceroy Iturrigaray wrote to him on the subject as follows: "Bearing in mind how useful must be for the preaching of the Light of the Gospel to the pagans of your province the founding of a Mission as proposed by the late governor in the locality called Calahuasa on the spot named Lajalupe (Alajulapu rather), I have resolved that

[1] Fr. Tápis to Fr. Lasuén, October 23, 1798; Fr. Tápis to Gov. Arrillaga, June 30, 1803. *Santa Barbara Mission Archives.*

EARLIEST ILLUSTRATION OF MISSION SANTA INES. AUTHOR UNKNOWN, 1875.

it should be effected; and I have given orders to the Minister of this Treasury to pay to the síndico of the Apostolic College of San Fernando the $1,000 which the Reglamento assigns.

I also charge the Rev. Fr. Guardian of said College to send at an opportune time two Religious (missionaries) who merit his confidence. I notify Your Honor so that you may be informed on the subject so far as concerns you; and so that you may provide security for this new establishment in accordance with your knowledge, and the troops that are to live there etc."[2]

Arrillaga from Loreto, Lower California, forwarded a copy of the foregoing letter, which he knew would cause rejoicing, to Fr. Lasuén under date of April 29, 1803, and remarked as follows: "Complying with the preceding Order, I am ready to provide the assistance that depends upon my judgment; but, before naming the guards, I beg Your Paternity to be pleased to manifest to me what you know about the pagans who exist in the locality of Calahuasa and its immediate vicinity, or at a distance, and whether the number of troops, five men under a corporal, regularly assigned, is sufficient or not for the protection of the Mission; for, inasmuch as I lack the necessary knowledge of the site, I should not want to err in such an interesting matter."[3]

When the governor's letter arrived, the aged Fr. Lasuén had just died at Mission San Carlos on June 26, 1803. Fr. Estévan Tápis, his successor in the office of Presidente of the Missions, therefore, made the reply. Concerning the Indians of the District, he repeated the report made to Fr. Lasuén in 1798, which was reproduced on the preceding pages. "With regard to the number of troops," he said, "which may be necessary to guard the new Mission, I have to say, that this Mission will be less visited than the others, because it will be necessary to pass the Sierra of Mescaltitlan, or to go by way of the rancho of the Ortegas. The one as well as the other is

---

[2] *Santa Barbara Archives.*
[3] *Santa Barbara Archives.*

more inconvenient and difficult than the road along the beach
to Monterey. Although the Gentiles, whom I found in the
district about Alajulapu, are not excessively numerous, it is
to be noted that there is communication between these rancherias and the savages nearest to the Tulares, especially the
large rancherias named Atsililihu and Sihuicon. These Gentiles are of a bad disposition. They are turbulent, inclined to
commit murder in a most treacherous way and from merely
superstitious motives. During the month of April, 1801, a
certain Lihuiasu with about six companions from the two
rancherias mentioned came in the night time to set fire to
Eljman, a small rancheria which lay two leagues from Tegueps,
and about six leagues from Santa Barbara. He killed five
persons and wounded two others, solely because the Gentiles
of Eljman were relatives or friends of Temiacucat, the chief
of the Cuyamu Rancheria belonging to Dos Pueblos on the
seashore, whom they regarded as the author of the epidemic
of the *dolor de costado*, which at that time took the lives of
many Indians.

"A little later the same savage killed another Indian in his
own rancheria. A little more than two months ago, the same
Lihuiasu with ten companions went to kill, not far from San
Luis Obispo, a woman. For this inhumanity and others of the
kind they had no other motive than that he had been paid for
it. After the assassinations committed at Eljman, the Gentiles
of the mountains lived in constant dread on account of the
threats made against them by Lihuiasu. The Gañames of
this Mission (Santa Barbara) to the number of forty persons,
who were in the Sierra of Saccaya, distant from here about
fifteen leagues, getting out timber for 48 houses that were
under construction for as many neophyte families, in April
last had to arm themselves with bows and arrows for defense,
in case that said bloodthirsty savage attempted some assault
against them, as they feared in consequence of the notification
which a Gentile nephew of the said Lihuiasu gave them.

"All that has been said, and other similar instances which
might be added, make it clear that those savages, who may be

called neighbors to those of Alajulapu, are in a constant fer-
ment, the cause of which is their false notion that deaths, even
natural deaths, result from witchcraft and poisons, and that
the scarcity of rain and of seeds proceed from certain men who
among them are regarded as gods of the waters, and of the
good or bad crops.

"If Your Honor, after seeing this information, judge it expedient that the guard of the Mission of Alajulapu should be
considerable, and larger than the ordinary guard of a corporal
and five men, while time and experience demonstrate whether
or not there is need of more troops than in other missions,
your opinion will be in conformity with mine; but I do not
pretend this to be decisive; for I manifest it merely in order
to yield to the wishes of Your Honor, and in order to cooperate so far as possible with the spirit which animates you.
—Fr. Estévan Tápis."[4]

Under date of September 26, 1803, Fr. Guardian Thomas
de Pangua of the College of San Fernando declared that a
guard of six men was not sufficient for the safety of the Mission with so many hostile Indians near.[5]

Preparations were now made for the ceremony of founding
the Mission. This eventually took place. The exact account
of the proceedings rendered to Gov. Arrillaga by Fr. Tápis
himself reads as follows: "Praised be Jesus!—My Dear Governor:—I have the happy satisfaction to inform Your Honor
that on this date, the Day of the Wounds of our holy Father
St. Francis, in this place called by the natives *Alajulapu* distant from the rancheria of Calahuasa about two leagues,
about midway between the Missions of Santa Barbara and
Purisima Concepcion, away from the ocean about three
leagues, with the assistance of the lieutenant of the cavalry
and commander of the royal presidio of Santa Barbara, Don
Raymundo Carrillo, the RR. FF. Fr. Marcelino Cipres,
missionary of Mission San Luis Obispo, Fr. José Antonio
Calzada and Fr. Romualdo Gutiérrez destined for this estab-

---

4 *Santa Barbara Archives.*
5 *Santa Barbara Archives.*

THE FIRST AUTHENTIC ETCHING, BY HENRY CHAPMAN FORD, 1883.

lishment, the soldiers from this garrison, various white persons, many neophytes from the said Missions of Santa Barbara and Purisima, and more than 200 Gentiles of both sexes and of all ages; I blessed water, the place, and the great cross which we planted and venerated. We sang immediately the Litany of All Saints in the *enramada* (brushwood shelter) intended for the church until the one under construction of adobe is completed. I then sang the High Mass and preached to the people *de razon*, and the neophytes, to the Gentiles, through an interpreter, I gave to understand the object of this establishment, and animated them to enter the fold of holy Church, outside of which there is no salvation. We concluded the function by singing the *Te Deum Laudamus* with the respective prayers and orations in thanksgiving. Finally a *Salve* was sung to the most holy Virgin.

"After a short while, the pagans presented twenty-seven children, that is to say, twelve male and fifteen female children, and desired that holy Baptism be administered to them. I yielded to the pious supplication. I blessed the (baptismal) water, and in the forenoon I baptized the male children between one and six years of age, Don Raymundo Carrillo being sponsor. In the afternoon I baptized the female children, who ranged between six months and seven years of age. Francisca, wife of retired Sergeant José Maria Ortega, was godmother.

"On this same day fifteen male adults clothed themselves and were enlisted for catechetical instruction. Among them were the three chiefs of the three rancherias Calahuasa, Soctonocmu, and Ahuama. The rest of the pagans offered to become Christians when they had finished gathering the wild seeds, in their language called *Tayujas*, the harvesting of which would conclude in fifteen days.

"Thus possession was taken of this site, and it was dedicated in honor of the glorious Virgin and Martyr, Saint Agnes. In this manner the Mission under this sacred title, was begun, in conformity with the higher orders of His Excellency, the Viceroy of New Spain, Don José de Iturrigaray, and of Your

Honor.—God keep your Honor many years in His holy grace.
—Mission Santa Inés, September 17, 1804.—B. S. M. of
Your Honor. Your most affectionate servant and chaplain,
Fr. Estévan Tápis.—To the Lieutenant Colonel, Commander
and Inspector, Don José J. de Arrillaga."[6]

An adobe church was built in the first year, but all details
regarding it are lacking. The missionaries were not nearly
so independent on this subject, nor on any other, as un-
friendly writers would have the public believe. This will
be made clear by quoting a letter addressed to the Fr. Presidente Lasuén by the Viceroy. It reads: "In the royal cédula
of December 22, 1800, his Majesty among other things gives
warning that the missionaries of this province of New California, as well as those of Lower California, should not undertake the building of new churches in the pueblos of their
charge without consulting the government of the peninsula.
They will thus avoid the inconveniences that for lack of
means for paying the cost the Indians might suffer in their
maintenance by obliging many to labor, whilst they have but
few for the work of providing subsistence. I communicate
this to Your Reverence, asking and charging you to have
your subjects observe the royal resolution stated."

To Fr. Lasuén this warning must have seemed uncalled
for. Without oppressing the neophytes in the least, he had
built a church at Mission San Diego, and had boasted of its
beauty to Fr. Serra twenty-two years before. Likewise other
missionaries had utilized the building of churches as training
schools for the mechanics without arousing any discontent
whatever. However, Fr. Lasuén in a circular dated April 3,
1802, brought Viceroy Marquina's communication of November 5, 1801, to the attention of the friars, and commanded
them to observe it. All the Fathers, according to regulations,
signed the circular on its reception without comment.[7]

[6] *Santa Barbara Archives.*
[7] *San Diego Mission*, 106-107; 113-114. *Santa Barbara Archives.*

At the close of the year, December 31, 1804, the baptismal register contained the names of 112 Indian converts of all ages. The first little girl, baptized on the day of the founding, was named for the patron saint of the Mission—Inés.

Besides these baptized here at the time, neophytes from other Missions, notably from Santa Barbara and Purisima Concepcion, were permitted to join the new establishment, probably because they originated in that district. Thus it is that the *padron*, or Mission Roll, at the end of the same year 1804 contained the names of 116 male and 109 female Indians who lived under the shadow of the Cross at Santa Inés.

At the end of 1806, including 132 neophytes from Santa Barbara Mission and 145 from Purisima Concepcion Mission, 229 male and 341 female Indian converts, in all 570, were on the roll of Mission Santa Inés. 253 adults, 76 children of neophytes, 38 children of pagans and catechumens, and four white children, or in all 371 had been baptized at the Mission. 100 Indian couples had been married or received the marriage blessing for marriages already contracted in the pagan state; and 118 neophytes, including 45 from the two Missions named, had died.

CHAPTER II.

Before proceeding with the narrative, it will be in order to describe the characteristics and habits of the Indians in this region of Santa Inés Mission. We have a complete description from the hands of the two Fathers stationed there in 1814, written in obedience to a demand from the Spanish Government. This, on October 6, 1811, sent a list of thirty-two questions to the Bishop of Sonora, who referred the document to the Fr. Presidente of the Missions. Each Mission received a copy with the request to reply to each question in full. The result was the description reproduced here. Only the questions are omitted, as they may be inferred from the replies.

1. The population of this Mission is divided into Europeans, who are the missionaries, Indians, and *gente-de-razon.* By the latter term all are understood who are not Indians, and these reduce themselves to one corporal and five leather-jacket soldiers (the first and four soldiers are married,) who compose the guard of this Mission; and six families who reside in a ranch distant a little more than three leagues from this Mission. Among them all there is no negro whatever, but they are as to color mixed, and others of white color. All regard themselves as Americans. Most of them have been born in this province, their parents having come here from Lower California and from Sonora.

2. The Indians of this Mission are natives of the surrounding rancherias, children of pagan parents, with the exception of those born in the Mission during the nine years since its founding.

3. The language generally spoken is the native one of the country; but some understand and speak Spanish.

4. Commonly the husbands love their wives, when both are young, and if the wives are of use; but when they are ill, especially with habitual illness, and they have no children,

they love them little. When reaching a certain age, about forty years, they love and assist their wives, be they ill or be they well. The mothers have particular love for their children, the fathers not so much. One and the other give the children very little education; and it can be said that they receive it only in spiritual as well as temporal things, from the RR. FF. Missionaries, who apply them, when the children are found to be at suitable age, to duties of tilling the soil, to carpenter work, to shoemaking, to masonry or bricklaying, to weaving, and to other mechanical arts necessary in the Mission.

5. There has not been observed in these Indians any disposition for complaining, nor for hatred against the Europeans and Americans, whom alone they know by the term of *gente-de-razon*, and for whom they have more inclination and affection than aversion.

6. For the last four months boys have been selected to learn to read Castilian, and they offer hopes that they will not delay to read to perfection. This may lead to understanding and speaking Castilian. Generally it was not spoken, nor understood by the neophytes because they have come from paganism, most of them adults, and among them many at a very advanced age.

7. The virtues found among them are enduring and suffering hardships, infirmities, and adversities, humility, obedience, and submission. In both sexes are charity and compassion; but few are generous, perhaps for lack of means to manifest generosity.

8. Inasmuch as most of these neophytes have been raised amidst the superstitions of paganism, there are some, especially old men and old women, who as yet are not undeceived about them. When the rancherias were inhabited by pagans, there were seen in various places bunches of feathers or plumes, fastened upon a pole, which could be called their places of worship. There they would cast seeds and beads in order to secure harvests of acorns and of other seeds which the soil produces naturally, and these constituted their daily nourishment. These and other similar cults would be directed

to an invisible being, which they pictured to themselves with ridiculous notions as the author of the rains, of the seeds and fruits, and of health, and of good luck in fishing, in the chase, etc. Since all these people have been baptized those bunches of plumes have disappeared; some are encountered in the country outside or in the mountains. Their devotees are careful to do in secret what they formerly did in public.

9. The native language of the neophytes of this Mission has a catechism of the Christian Doctrine without the approbation of the Rt. Rev. Bishop, and it is in use every day, alternating with the one in the Castilian language.

10. No inclination towards idolatry is observed in these neophytes.

11. These Indians, the men before they were baptized, went about entirely naked; the women with less indecency. They lived without king and without law. They maintained themselves with acorns, seeds, and herbs, which the land produces of itself. They knew no other labor than that of the dance, play, and one or another hunting deer, rabbits, squirrels, ducks, etc., and that of fishing if he were a *playano*— lived on the ocean shore. In gathering their fruits and similar wild seeds, they were continually in danger of being attacked by the bears and bitten by snakes. Now they go dressed with decency without distinction of the sexes, or ages. They are subject to God, and to the sovereign through the governors and missionaries, who represent Him. They now subsist on wheat, corn, peas, beef, free from the perils in which they saw themselves before; and they work respectively in the shops and at whatever is to be done at the Mission in which they are occupied; and this is the advantage which results from having become Christians.

12. At this Mission the neophytes do not celebrate compacts nor stipulations for their matrimonial contracts, nor do the candidates offer any service to the parents of the bride. When any one desires to marry he presents himself to the missionary Father, pointing out the person with whom he seeks to contract marriage. The missionary ascertains whether

the marriage is agreeable to the parents of both parties. When these and their parents consent, and no canonical impediment results from the investigation, they marry with all the formalities of the Church.

13. Generally the curative method employed in their illness consists in the deception which the sick undergo, whose authors are some Indians who in the pagan state were regarded as healers. These make the sick believe that their illness is caused by some feather, claw of a leopard, a chip, hairs, etc., which they have in the body. The patient, desirous of obtaining health, pays such frauds well, who with their arts and crafts pretend to extract the feather, etc., from the body, but in reality from their own hand. So the patient keeps his illness, but not his *abalórios* and other things which are given to the healer in payment for the *mentira*—the deception. Other healers have the method of extracting blood from the patient without any incision in the body. So the sick ignorantly believe, as the blood comes from the mouth of the same healer, who keeps in it a sore or wound; and when there is occasion to suck blood (so they call this cure) he takes into his mouth warm water, and pretending to suck or extract blood from the body of the patient, he takes it from his own mouth, mixed with water. This remedy is a *cura lo todo*— cure-all, leaving always the sickness as it was, as must be supposed. From this it must be inferred that these neophytes have little or no knowledge of the curative powers of the plants, roots, etc. The only relief which they have in their afflictions comes to them from the missionary Fathers, who, when they recognize the infirmity, apply those remedies which they judge could be useful and not harmful to them. The Indians make no use of hot water baths, because there is none at the Mission nor in its proximity.

14. The seasons of the year these Indians know and distinguish from the cold and rains of the winter, from the heat of the summer, from the first wild seeds that appear in the spring, and from the acorns of live-oak and the oak which are

FIRST PHOTOGRAPH OF MISSION SANTA INES, BY WATKINS.

in season in the fall, and by other wild seeds and fruits which occur at various periods of the year. They never had nor used a calendar.

15. The meals they take in a day, are three regularly: in the morning before going out to work, at noon, and at evening. The dishes which they prepare are from wheat, corn, peas, beef, seasoned according to taste, without forgetting their ancient foods of acorns, herbs, wild seeds, when they are in season or occasion offers. Inasmuch as the harvests of the said grains have been abundant in these last years, there is no account kept of what they consume. Every family receives from the common storeroom in the presence of some *alcalde* or *regidor*, wheat, corn, or peas in the quantity which it requires; and for a little more than 600 persons, old and young, which the Mission counts, there are slaughtered sixteen large and selected head of cattle every week.

16. These neophytes do not use fermented drinks; but they use a confection of wild tobacco and lime, which when it is chewed strengthens them, as they say; but if they go to excess it intoxicates them, as happened with some.

17. These neophytes have not worshipped either the sun or the moon.

18. These Indians possess no knowledge whatever of their primitive ancestors; nor likewise any information or tradition from which part or from which direction their ancestors came to settle here.

19. At their burials they employ no other ceremonial than that of the Church; and the whole mourning at the death of a neophyte is reduced to the wailing of the relatives in the house where one died or in his own house.

20. In the few transactions which the neophytes have it seems they are faithful enough. Only at their games, innocent in themselves, are some who let not the occasion pass which presents itself to cheat their opponent.

21. Likewise they do not overlook the occasion to tell lies,

if with the lie they can exculpate themselves of a fault or guilt of which they are accused; but when convicted they confess the truth.

22. Among these neophytes rarely one has any money. Seeds they all have equally in common and sufficiently; therefore there is little lending among them. Beads or abalórios is the money that circulates among these people, and of these they lend here and there without profit, and without more agreement than that it be returned in kind.

23. In planting grain no contracts whatever are made. They are done in common by direction of the missionary Fathers on the land of the Mission. For common consumption the rations of wheat, corn, or peas, are distributed weekly to the families.

24. These Indians are not inclined to anger much less to cruelty; nor do they among themselves employ any chastisements. The native parents themselves are incapable of chastising their sons, though these may have deserved it very much. In the matter of punishment, when there is necessity for inflicting it, they are subject to the missionary Fathers, provided the transgression be not a capital crime. If it be, officers of the sovereign apply the punishment.

25. These Indians in their pagan state never immolated human victims to their gods, nor have they any inclination for such horrible sacrifices. In the burials of their bodies they observe no particular ceremonial, as was said before; nor do they place food for them, nor do they burn them.

26. In this Mission there is no Indian who calls himself rich; but all may call themselves well-to-do, for all have what is sufficient for corporal subsistence by means of moderate labor to which the able-bodied and well apply themselves, as well for themselves as for the aged, the infants and the sick.

27. In this Mission there are no Indian *caciques* and governors; nor is there more distinction among them than of *alcaldes*, and *regidores* whom they elect annually, and they are

subject in political and economical matters to the missionary Fathers, and in criminal affairs to the government of the province.

28. The whole personal service of these Indians amounts to preparing, by the Indian who is cook, the meals for the missionary Fathers; to aiding them in the functions of the Church by some boys and in the administration of the Sacraments; these also serve in the house doing the little that is necessary and whatever turns up. Once in a while a female Indian is occupied in washing the tunic and other clothing which a Franciscan missionary may wear, and also what belongs to the Church. All these who would otherwise work for the Indian community, offer some service to the missionary Fathers; but the missionaries give their whole service to all, not only in spiritual things, but also in temporal matters. The one and the other gives it cheerfully—the Indians because they are dispensed from heavier work and daily eat the same food which the missionary Fathers eat; and the Fathers because they know it is their duty, and in accomplishing it they have a well-founded hope of an eternal recompense.

Fr. Estevan Tapis,

29. In their pagan state these Indians neither knew nor used any other musical instruments than a wooden tube which resembled the flute, open at both ends, and produced a buzzing sound disagreeable to the ear; also a whistle of the bone of a bird. In the songs which they possessed in their language, that is to say, in which they articulated some kind of words in their idiom, and which they used at their dances, there was nothing particular save the evenness of the chant, although there were many who chanted at the same time.

They no longer hear such chants nor instruments, but in their place are heard devout songs and harmonized instruments. The *violin*, the *baja de violon*, the violin (instruments made by the neophytes themselves, as also the *tambora*), the sweet German flute, the trompa, the bandola, are those they know and use in the functions of the Church. They are fond of music, and they learn easily by memory the sonatas which they hear, or which are taught them.

3(). These Indians have not had any man distinguished for letters or arms.

31. When they were pagans they had no idea of eternity, of reward, of punishment, of final judgment, heaven, purgatory, and hell. Now that they are Christians they have a knowledge of everything Religion teaches them.

32. The neophytes here go about decently clad. The men wear the woolen shirt or over-all with sleeves. It reaches down below the thigh. They also wear the sapeta or taparabo —or breechcloth. In Sonora this is a piece of cloth with which the Indians cover their loins all around. It is of cotton or wool about a yard and a half long and something more than half a yard wide. It measures less long and less wide for boys. In addition, they wear the blanket. The women wear the chemise, the petticoat of wool and the blanket. All this wearing apparel is made in the weaving rooms of the Mission by the neophytes selected for this kind of manufacture.

Mission Santa Inés, March 8th, 1814.

Fr. Estévan Tápis.—Fr. Francisco Xavier Uria.

---

*Only thirty-two questions were answered because the subject matter of the others were included already in the report.

CHAPTER III.

Considerable building activities were reported for the very
first year. According to the Annual Report sent to the Fr.
Presidente at the end of 1804, a row of buildings was constructed which measured 84 varas,[1] or about 232 feet in length,
seven varas or about 19 feet in width, and seven varas also
in height. This wing contained the temporary church, 31
varas or about 86 feet long, the sacristy five varas or 14 feet
long, the habitation of the Fathers 10½ varas or about 29
feet long, and a granary 37½ varas, or about 103 feet long.
This portion was commenced six months before the formal
founding of the Mission, with the aid of Missions Santa Barbara and Purisima Concepcion. The latter was then situated
on the southern end of what is now Lompoc. The walls of the
structures at Santa Inés, hence of the church also, were of
adobe and about 30 inches thick; but the roofing consisted of
poles over which sticks were laid side by side. The whole was
then covered with adobe soil.

In 1805 another row of buildings was erected. This measured 52 varas or about 145 feet in length, 19 feet in width and
19 feet in height. The walls were of adobe, and of the same
thickness as those of the preceding structures, but it was
roofed with tiles. Tiles were also placed on the structure
measuring 84 varas of the previous year 1804. The report for
this year, dated December 31, was signed by Fathers Calzada
and Gutierrez.

At the close of 1806, Fathers Calzada and Luis Gil report
that under their supervision during the year the neophytes
had constructed a row of adobe buildings 132 Spanish yards

---

[1] A vara or Spanish yard is equal to about 33½ inches.

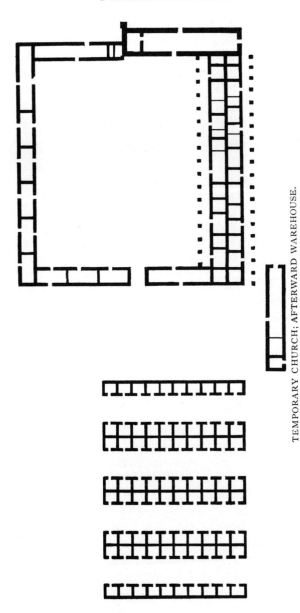

TEMPORARY CHURCH; AFTERWARD WAREHOUSE.

GROUND PLAN OF MISSION SANTA INES, AND OF THE NEOPHYTE VILLAGE BEFORE REVOLT 1824.

(varas) or about 368 feet long, seven varas wide and seven varas high. This structure, doubtless a wing of the quadrangle, was roofed with tiles. The walls were one adobe and a half thick like the others, i. e.,about thirty inches. In order to protect the walls against rains a gallery or corridor was built which was 27 varas or about 75 feet long and seven varas or about 19 feet wide. The roofing was covered with tiles.

In this year, too, an expedition equipped for a survey of the country to the east, or interior of California, set out from Santa Barbara on July 19, and in the evening of the same day reached Mission Santa Inés. It was composed of a lieutenant, a corporal, and a number of soldiers. Fr. José Maria de Zalvidea accompanied the men as chaplain and chronicler. Next morning after holy Mass the company continued the march to the Tulares. For the route and incidents of note see *The Missions and Missionaries,* vol. ii, pp. 647; 701-702.

In 1807 new habitations for the missionaries were begun, but not completed till the following year. The dimensions are not given in the report of that year.

In 1810 five double houses, apparently of two rooms, were built for as many soldiers and their families. A storehouse and a guardhouse for them were also erected. The dimensions were again forgotten.

An important feature concerning this Mission and that of Mission Purisima Concepcion was reported by Fr. Mariano Payeras of Purisima as follows for 1810: "In order to facilitate and shorten for the public and for the mail-carriers the road between Mission Santa Inés and this of Purisima, and from this to that of San Luis Obispo, two roads have been run through the mountain of this river, each forty paces wide." Six years later the same Fr. Payeras reported: "On this day, January 10, 1816, a road was surveyed from the door of this Mission of Purisima to that of Mission Santa Inés, and it was found to be six leagues, and three quarters of a league and 619 yards long."

In 1811 a house for the mayordomo, 25 varas long and six varas wide was erected. It was like the rest of the buildings and roofed with tiles.

A great task was achieved in 1812. During this year 80 adobe houses were built each of which measured six by six and one-half varas. These structures doubtless constituted the neophyte village or rancheria, of which the foundations may still be easily traced. A drawing accompanying this shows the location and system employed.

At the end of this year also, Fathers Uria and Olbés had to report some mishaps that befell the Mission, which fortunately could not compare with the disaster that visited the neighboring Mission of Purisima. On December 31, 1812, the Fathers write: "On December 21, 1812, at about 10 o'clock in the morning occurred two earthquakes at an interval of a quarter of an hour. The first made a considerable aperture in one corner of the church; the second shock threw down the said corner, and a quarter of the new houses contiguous to the church collapsed to the foundation. All the thin walls of the upper parts of new houses fell down, demolished all the tiles, and opened many a main wall. All remain serviceable, however, if no greater damage occurs. So far as circumstances permitted all the buildings have been repaired."

In 1813, Fathers Tápis and Uria, on December 31st, report that the habitation of the missionaries was lowered, the flat roof taken down and replaced with a gable roof covered with tiles. This structure was plastered inside and outside.

In the same year a long narrow building was erected to serve as a church, because the church erected at the founding of the Mission had been rendered unserviceable by the earthquake of 1812. It faced the north. The dimensions, outside measure, were—length from the front to the sanctuary— about 100 feet; sanctuary to vestry wall—25 feet; adobe wall—15 inches; vestry under the same roof—19 feet. In all, therefore, 145 feet. Width—about 19 feet; walls all around, four feet thick, were about 12 feet high inside, and were supported by buttresses of stone laid in mortar.

The gable roof was covered with tile.

Besides the front door, there was a side door which opened to the west on the Indian village, along the front of which this new, but temporary church, was largely situated. There was also a door in the vestry which opened on the eastside. This structure was used till the new or present much larger church building had been finished, that is to say, to the year 1817. Thereafter this temporary church structure was utilized as a commissariat for provisions, which were distributed every week. It was still standing in 1855. Decay then set in and the commissioners took down the tiles and used them in their own buildings, as Fernandito relates. Collapse followed, and left but a heap of adobe to tell the tale.

Fr Fran.co Xavier Uria

In 1814 the grounds were excavated for the stone foundation of a new church, already mentioned. Under the direction of the two missionaries, Fathers Uria and Ulibarri, the neophytes were employed at their jobs all through the years 1815 and 1816. On December 31, 1816, the happy Friars reported that the really grand edifice was completed, and that the workmen, all Indians, were busy plastering and decorating the interior. A belfry was also built. When all preparations had been made, the new temple was blessed and dedicated on Friday, July 4th, 1817. This date was probably chosen, because on that day the Franciscans everywhere celebrated the Feast of the Anniversary of the Dedication of All the Churches of the Order. It might reasonably be supposed that the two Fathers had described the solemnities minutely; but besides stating the date of the dedication and blessing in their report of December 31, 1817, as above, only one other allusion is made to the event in the baptismal register in connection with a Baptism. The entry is therefore reproduced entire. It reads as follows: "No. 1014. On July 10, 1817, in the church

of this Mission of Santa Inés, which was blessed on the 4th.
day of the same month and year with solemn functions, I
solemnly baptized a male infant born in the previous night,
son of José Maria Jauinat and Cuitaquia, whom I gave the
name Nicolas Inés, etc.—Fr. Francisco Xavier Uria."

The church building, the interior of which resembles tha t
of Santa Barbara, according to the report of December 31,
1816, measured fifty varas, or about 139 feet in length, 9
varas or about 25 feet in width, and 9 varas in height. The
walls, two and one-half feet thick, were of adobe, except on
the southside, where the wall was veneered with burnt brick.
The sacristy in the rear, but under the same roof with the
church, was as wide as the main structure, but only six varas
deep. Back of the sacristy was a room for keeping the utensils
used on certain feast days. Its dimensions were seven by six
and one-half varas. There was another room eight by six and
a half varas, the purpose of which was not specified. All these
structures had beams of pine timber, and all were roofed with
tiles.

It is to be noted that the present church edifice occupies
the northeast corner of a quadrangle which with the church
faces toward the east. The original dimensions of the quadrangle were as follows: North to south—350 feet; from east
to west, beginning at the southeast corners, about 345, or
possibly 350; thence from the southwest corner toward the
north—about 335 feet; thence the wall runs east just into the
centre of the rear of the church building addition, which was
a store room, lower in height than the church, —about 118
feet.

The outside walls of the quadrangle were the walls of the
shops, and ran from the southeast corner back to the west;
thence to the north the walls were twenty feet high in order
to protect the buildings inside against the tremendous winds
coming from the southwest. These buildings along the walls
in the interior were also roofed with tiles and plastered.

In 1817, besides the work on the church building, new
timbers were put in various structures. The habitations of

INTERIOR VIEW OF MISSION SANTA INES

the soldiers and the guardhouse had to be rebuilt. A corridor was added. A large corral completed the building activities of the year.

Various beautiful vestments and other church goods were acquired and reported since the year 1813, although after 1811, owing to the Hidalgo revolt, no assistance of any kind could be obtained from Mexico. Here as elsewhere the Fathers took particular care to have the articles pertaining to divine worship in perfect condition and complete. It would be tedious to enumerate all that was secured through interested friends and through barter with merchants. Many of the linen goods were made by the girls and women at the Mission, and they also kept in repair what served for divine services.

Some of the church goods, however, deserve particular mention. In 1817, for instance, the Fathers report having secured a goldplated chandelier with eight arms. In 1818 a Way of the Cross was put in. The fourteen pictures were paintings on canvas.

Building operations continued to provide for the necessities of the neophyte population. For instance, in 1820 a grist mill was erected of masonry, for grinding wheat, corn, etc. Its dimensions were seven varas or nineteen feet in length and five and a half varas or fifteen feet in width. It was roofed with tiles.

In 1821 a fulling mill for the cleansing of cloth woven at the Mission was constructed of burnt brick. The dimensions are given as six varas in length and five varas in width. This building, too, was roofed with tiles.

In 1823 a building was put up for the storing of all kinds of supplies pertaining to the cowherders. It measured 15 by six and one-half varas, or 44 by 18 feet.

Thus far, beginning of the year 1824, life at Mission Santa Inés had continued peacefully enough under the energetic administration of Fr. Francisco Xavier Uria. He had been in charge since December 1808, and during that period he had transformed the Mission into an active and thriving community of neophytes. The converts had steadily increased, as the baptismal register demonstrates. He had found the number of Baptisms on record to be 441 on December 8, 1808, but by February 17, 1824, when Fr. Uria baptized here for the last time, 1227 entries had been made. From the beginning of October, 1820, he was alone, as Fr. Ulibarri, who suffered from ill health, had been transferred to Purisima Concepcion, and had made entries at Santa Inés only twice, thereafter, December 4, 1818, and November 20, 1819. The neophyte Indian community at Santa Inés at the end of 1823 consisted of 217 male adults, 84 male children, 210 female adults and 53 girls, hence 301 male Indians and 263 female Indians, or 564 altogether.

At this state in its history, the usual peace and tranquillity was suddenly disturbed by a revolt of some of the younger Indians, but details are missing. Even the real occasion for the uprising is clouded in mystery. The remote causes, however, stand out clear enough. They are described in a letter which the Fr. Guardian of the College of San Fernando de Mexico addressed to Don Lucas Alaman, Minister of Relations, on July 5, 1825. "It may be said with truth," he writes, "that the Missions alone, or the labor (sudor) of the down-hearted neophytes, have sustained the troops since 1810. The Indians complain bitterly that they are toiling so that the soldiers may eat, and that they receive nothing for their toil (sudor) and labor. This discontent, despite every means and ways which the missionaries employ to lighten the burdens, it very likely was that resulted in the revolt of the Indians of the Missions of Santa Barbara, Purisima, and Santa Inés. In one they burnt even the granaries with the grain; the other two have been plundered, and the missionaries were unable to prevent it. There have been various deaths in the one and the other party owing to the resistence which the Indians made to the troops who hastened to the relief of the Mission, and finally the Indians fled to the regions of the pagans, the Tulares, about forty leagues distant. The Fr. Presidente of the Missions then took a hand in the trouble. With sweetness and gentleness, and armed with a general amnesty, he suc-

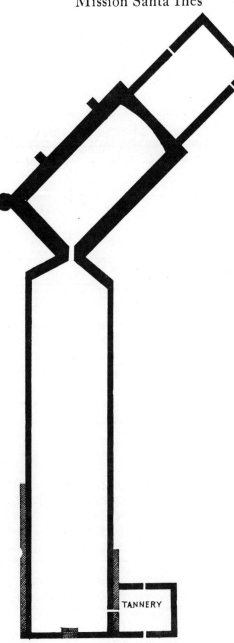

TANNERY

DIAGRAM OF WONDERFUL WATER WORKS SYSTEM.
BUILT DURING THE ADMINISTRATION OF FR. FRANCISCO X. URIA.

ceeded in persuading the majority, and brought them back
with him to their respective Missions. However, the bad
example given, the same Indians may repeat their designs,
and, what God may forbid, the revolt may become general,
and so the province will be ruined; for, if the Indians flee to
the pagans, all will perish, troops and settlers, because if the
soldier must eat, he must have it from the labor of the Indian,
inasmuch as the settlers for shame are so lazy and shiftless at
work, that they too will not have anything to eat if the Indian
does not work.

"The revolt was not against the missionaries; on the contrary, the revolting Indians wanted to have the Fathers go
along with them, and told them that they would care for
them. The revolt came about because they were made to
work in order to maintain the troops, and nothing was given
them in payment, as they said. To this was added, to the increased disgust of the Indians, the extraordinary contributions
imposed by the assembly of the province, which the Missions,
which is the same as the Indians, have to pay in cash, and
everything else they had to pay in kind. In every way, Señor,
those unhappy neophytes are harassed, and they have no
other choice than to appeal through me to the protection of
the Most Excellent President of the Federation (Mexico).
I supplicate Your Excellency with the most respectful submission to deign to consider my reflections and supplications,
in order that, your compassionate heart having been moved
in favor of the poor Indians, steps may be taken that the procurator be granted the payment of some of the drafts, that
relief may be sent to the neophytes, at least some goods of
prime necessity; for without such aid it is impossible for the
procurator to secure the goods since he has not wherewith to
pay for them. This would most probably result in the good
effect of decreasing somewhat the discontent, etc.—Fr.
Baldomero Lopez, Guardian."[2]

The immediate cause for the outbreak, according to Bancroft, who is not certain, however, was the flogging of a neo-

---

[2] *Archbishop's Archives.* No. 1739.

phyte from Purisima Mission by order of Corporal Cota. Details are not known. At all events, the neophytes of Mission Santa Inés and of Mission Purisima Concepcion conspired to take revenge on the soldiers. The affray began on Saturday afternoon, February 21. Armed with bows and arrows a number of Indians attacked the guards, who seem to have hastily retreated to a building in the rear of the church from where they fired at their assailants. The result was that two Indians were killed. Both were from Mission Purisima and named Sebastian and Cipriano respectively. More about them in the chapter on the Mission Books. The infuriated Indians then set fire to the building in which it seems the guards and Fr. Uria had taken refuge, probably for the purpose of forcing the guards into the open; but the fire spread to the roof of the vestry in the rear of the church. At sight of the danger to the house of God, the rage of the rebels subsided. At any rate, they did all they could to prevent the destruction of the sacred edifice. They succeeded, though not before that part of the roof which covered the vestry was consumed.

The besieged guards held their post till the next day, when Sergeant Anastasio Carrillo with a small force of soldiers arrived from Santa Barbara. Then the rebel Indians retired to the second last row in the village and barricaded themselves against the soldiers, who set fire to the structures and thus dislodged the malcontents. Whether any of the rebels there were killed, is not known; but the row of destroyed buildings was never rebuilt. For a long time thereafter its ruins reminded the younger Indians, who had allowed themselves to be inveigled into the conspiracy, of their folly. One reason for their treachery it was claimed also concerned Fr. Uria, who was a great joker, but for all that insisted on the observance of the moral law, which young Indians are likely to disregard occasionally. The Tulares, inhabited by pagan savages, were not so far away that intercourse was difficult. It is quite probable that Fr. Uria interfered with their unlawful pastimes, and thus incurred the wrath of some of them, as in the case of Father Quintana at Vera Cruz. When such a fever comes over the animal Indian it is prudent to mistrust him. At all events, Fr. Uria did not return to Santa Inés, but was appointed for Mission Soledad.

A story was circulated about Fr. Uria at the time of the revolt. It was asserted that he jumped through a window and ran down the bluff for the purpose of escaping to Santa Barbara. Soon after two Indians discovered his trail and followed it. When they came up with him they wanted to shoot him down with arrows, but Fr. Uria turning discharged a pistol at one of them who fell dead, while the other escaped. Then Fr. Uria made his way to Santa Barbara. This story is manifestly untrue. Fr. Uria with the soldiers, though besieged with them, was safe enough, and had but to wait for the arrival of the troops coming from Santa Barbara. Furthermore, the Fathers never went armed. It is not likely that any of the soldiers would have given him a pistol, which the guards needed themselves. With it he could have been of much use to the guards right where they were behind their barricade. Anyhow, there is no evidence that Fr. Uria endeavored to escape in the way imagined. He went to Santa Barbara in the company of the guards. Nor was he suspended for having killed an Indian even in self defence, as the Indians later fabled; for he immediately occupied himself with the duties of the ministry at Santa Barbara until transferred as missionary to Soledad.

After the revolt at Purisima had ceased, its missionary Fr. Antonio Rodriguez took up his residence at Mission Santa Inés till the end of June, 1824; for both he and Fr. Blas Ordaz made entries in the various Mission registers, Fr. Rodriguez for the last time on June 23rd, when he went to Mission San Luis Obispo.

As already indicated, Fr. Blas Ordaz succeeded Fr. Uria at Santa Inés. He began to make entries in the registers on March 6th, only two weeks after the uprising. As for the rebels, some of them joined the conspirators at Mission Purisma, where a regular battle was fought with more disastrous results. Others probably retired to the Tulares region and made common cause with the refugees from Mission Santa Barbara, where the outbreak had worse consequences. On March 21st, Fr. Blas notified Governor Argüello that a Russian had been seen with the Santa Barbara fugitives at the Rancho San Emígdio. It would seem clear from this that, unlike Mission Santa Barbara, Santa Inés was not abandoned at all, and that, in fact, the majority of the neophytes had nothing to do with the revolt.

In the annual report of December 31, 1824, Fr. Blas Ordaz wrote that during the rebellion in February, "with the exception of the church and the *convento* (front wing), all the workshops, the soldiers' barracks, and the habitations of the guards, were destroyed. The weaving rooms, however, the spinning rooms, the apartments of the girls or *monjério*, and a room in the front wing had been restored, and other rooms were being repaired. This shows that a serious conflagration had visited the Mission, and that much more than the vestry of the church had suffered, as commonly related by writers on the subject. Nine cassocks for altar boys were also destroyed before the desperate efforts of the Indians succeeded in saving the church. During the year, however, the cassocks were replaced by new ones.

CHAPTER IV.

Building operations and repairs were continued in 1825
and resulted in the erection of a new guardhouse with battle-
ment, a house for the corporal, a room for the harnesses, etc.,
a kitchen and pantry, a storeroom with wine cellar in the
main building, another kitchen and pantry, and a guest
room. Numerous church goods were also secured. The interior of the church was painted; three oil paintings in goldplated frames for the walls of the church were procured; and
twelve rugs for the sanctuary, etc., were obtained.

In 1826 the sacristy was re-roofed to make it correspond
with the roof of the church. Furthermore a house was built
for the mayordomo, besides three habitations, a kitchen, and
a sala or reception room.

In 1827 the vestry was painted inside, and a wardrobe put
in which had six drawers for vestments. A large crucifix with
suitable covering was obtained, and the altar linens were re-
plenished. This all goes to show that Fr. Blas Ordaz took
great interest in the beauty of the house of God, which dis-
proves much that was said against him, and will be considered later.

For 1828 no reports are extant; but 1829 saw four additional rooms built.

Robinson on occasion of his visit in 1829,[1] says: "The
Mission was governed by Father Blas Ordaz, who received
us with the accustomed cordiality of his hospitable Order.
The building we found much like that of Santa Barbara,
differing only in appearance of the church and the cleanliness
of its apartments. In front was a large brick enclosure or

[1] *Life in California*, Page 60.

declivity used for bathing and washing. To the right were the gardens and orchards filled with choice fruit trees. To the left were the Indian huts and tiled houses." It is nowhere stated when the brick structure, still extant, in front of the Mission was built. Most probably it dates from the time of Fr. Uria, before 1824. There is also a double reservoir about half a mile from the front of the Mission. All dates regarding this remarkable structure and about the aqueducts which led the water to the brick reservoir in front of the Mission are unfortunately missing.

Pattie claims to have vaccinated 900 people here early in 1828. As the Indian population consisted of only 455 souls, and there were not twenty whites, it is clear that Pattie erred as usual. More about him in our *Mission Dolores*.

In 1830 the soap factory was roofed.

In 1831 the whole main Mission building and the guard-house were whitewashed, which gave the establishment a pleasing aspect. In this year, too, Fr. Ordaz added to the vestry three precious albs, etc.

In 1832 a granary was made of the loft under the gable roof of the main building of the Mission. Two chests with drawers were placed in the sacristy, and a pair of rugs was procured "for the adornment of the sacristy." This was Fr. Ordaz's last contribution to the vestry and sanctuary, as far as reported; for with this year 1832 all official reports cease here as elsewhere. His successor, Fr. José J. Jimeno, on December 31, 1834, writes, however, that during the year a large crucifix had been erected on a suitable pedestal, in the cemetery.

The Mission lands of Santa Inés in 1822, according to Bancroft, between the two ranges of the sierra, extended seven to nine leagues from north to south, and five to thirteen leagues from east to west.[2] Within this district the land useful for cultivation or for pasturage was utilized for the benefit of the Indian community; but not nearly all was on the level

[2] Bancroft, vol. ii, pp. 581-582.

or fit for cultivation. Furthermore frosts, grasshoppers, and squirrels did much damage. Nevertheless, various ignorant writers are in the habit of attributing enormous wealth to the Missions. One of them, Rev. Walter Colton, a Protestant preacher, who in 1846-1848 served as justice of the peace at Monterey, in his *Three Years in California*, page 449, says of Mission Santa Inés: "Its property in 1823 was valued at $800,000." It is useless to make any remarks on such a wild statement. The inventories to be presented later and the annual reports reproduced in tabular form will enlighten the reader sufficiently.

Like all the Missions, after 1811 Mission Santa Inés had to contribute supplies and clothing, etc., for the maintenance of the troops at the garrisons, and it was often requested to furnish cash for the needs of the governors. Details are not available, but according to Bancroft,[3] Mission Santa Inés from 1822 to 1827 alone furnished as much as $10,767 worth of provisions and other supplies to the garrison at Santa Barbara, for which it never received a penny.[4]

Owing to the distance from the coast, and the inconveniences of travel across the sierras, visitors were few at Mission Santa Inés. For the morals of the neophytes the remoteness from the presidio was a blessing, because the soldiers of the garrisons were in bad repute with the missionaries, whose efforts for the temporal and spiritual well-being of their Indian wards the soldiers to a large extent nullified by their bad conduct. The five guards at Mission Santa Inés, however, appear to have been married, and to have conducted themselves well enough in 1830. At any rate, Fr. Ordaz in a letter to the alcalde of Santa Barbara, dated January 7, defended these soldiers, and declared that they were subordinate, did no damage whatever, and that all reports to the contrary were false.

On August 2, 1834, the legislative assembly illegally

---

[3] Bancroft, vol. ii, p. 582.

[4] See *Missions and Missionaries*, vol. iii, pp. 19; 68-70; 123-129; 151; 236; iv, 94; 132-135.

FRONT CORRIDOR OF MISSION SANTA INES

passed a decree secularizing the Missions of California. It was but a blind to cover up a gigantic scheme for robbing the neophytes of their property. Under this law, which the General Government of Mexico repudiated, in spiritual matters Santa Inés with Purisima became a curacy of the second class. The unsalaried missionary, heretofore in absolute charge of the neophyte affairs, spiritual as well as temporal, was graciously "relieved" of the burden of managing the temporalities, which were to be turned over to a hired administrator. The missionary for his maintenance was to receive $1,000 as salary to be paid from the Mission income like that of the new manager. This unnecessary salary for the administrator added to the burdens of the neophytes, who gained nothing whatever by the change; for they had to labor more than before in order to produce the salaries. For the time being the decree was not executed with regard to Mission Santa Inés. Fr. José J. Jimeno, who had succeeded Fr. Ordaz, kept in control of the temporalities without a salary as before. Ere long a change came about, however, and its story is as follows.

In April, 1836, Mariano Chico, the new governor arrived from Mexico and landed at Santa Barbara. From there he made the journey overland to Monterey, which he reached on May 1st. On May 3rd he took the oath of office. He soon made himself cordially despised and hated by all classes of people. The reasons therefore the reader will find in Volume iv of *The Missions and Missionaries*. Here we are concerned only with an incident that drew down Chico's wrath on Fr. José Jimeno and his brother, Fr. Antonio, who happened to visit the Mission at the time. On his way to Los Angeles from Monterey in June, 1836, Chico at noon on Friday the 10th, unexpectedly arrived at Mission Santa Inés. Besides the two Fathers named, Fr. Marcos de Vitoria was staying at the Mission. All three Fathers hastily ran out to welcome the governor. One opened the door of the carriage, another offered his hand, while Fr. José Jimeno expressed his regret that his ignorance of the time of the governor's arrival prevented the usual ceremonious reception accorded a governor.

The Mission bells, however, had been set a-ringing. The governor was then invited to dine at the Mission, but refused and at once continued on his way to Santa Barbara. He stopped for the night at the Ortega Rancho. Next day the unreasonable man informed Fr. Comisario Prefecto Narciso Durán at Mission Santa Barbara that he had announced himself at Mission Santa Inés through a cowboy!! and that he therefore was surprised when Fr. José Jimeno came out to meet him with the remark that no facilities could be afforded because his coming had not been known; that, although Fr. Vitoria was courteous, the Jimeno brothers had shown such disdain for him that he had to leave immediately. When Chico arrived at Santa Barbara, Fr. Durán visited him on the same day, but nothing that the Fr. Presidente could say satisfied the irate official. (Chico on June 20th, wrote to the General Government that "the Fr. Prefecto endeavored to excuse his brethren by alleging their inexperience in matters of etiquette.") Four days later, June 15th, Fr. Durán replied in writing to a question which Chico had propounded to him on the first day with regard to the duty of the Missions to furnish supplies. "In this paper," Fr. Durán wrote, "I shall not dwell upon what has occurred at Santa Inés . . . After all, those Fathers are my brethren, and I cannot but insist on acting as peacemaker until a complete pardon has been obtained from Your Honor in favor of these poor Religious, whose offense, I believe, could have been no more than surprise and oversight. I hope that you will hold the same opinion when you know them better."[5]

Instead of giving the Fathers the benefit of a doubt, at least, as a gentleman would have done, Chico let his anger make the incident an excuse for taking the management of Missions Santa Inés, San Buenaventura, and San Miguel, which had still remained in their charge, out of the hands of the Fathers. For that purpose he propounded a question which Fr. Duran courágeously answered, although he knew what the consequence would be. Without entering on the

---

[5] *The Missions and Missionaries*, vol. iii, pp. 21-22.

subject of the rights of the neophytes, which Fr. Durán had
set forth clearly, Chico replied on June 20, 1836, that Fr. José
Jimeno should surrender Mission Santa Inés to José Maria
Ramirez, in order that said citizen might administer the temporalities under the direction of the governor."[6] Chico in his
insane rage even wanted Fr. Durán banished from California,
and he actually sent orders to that effect to the alcalde of
Santa Barbara; but that is a story treated of in connection
with Mission Santa Barbara.

We have seen what explanation the Fathers at Mission
Santa Inés offered for not receiving Chico in the public and
official manner customary. They knew nothing of his intended
visit. This fact was corroborated by the sister-in-law of both
missionary Fathers, Mrs. Manuel Jimeno, who had been a
witness of what occurred.[7] Chico himself proved discourteous.
He claimed to have sent a *vaquero* (cowboy) picked up on the
road, to announce the coming of the governor. The cowboy
neglected to convey the verbal message. Surely this was not
a dignified way for sending a message even to poor missionaries. He should have notified the priests by a written note
if he desired a ceremonious reception. The truth is, Mariano
Chico was an illbred upstart whose conduct disgusted everybody to such a degree that he had to leave the territory an
exile before the lapse of three months.

The incident scarcely deserved the space accorded here;
but it touches the honor of the Franciscans whose hospitality
was proverbial. At least one writer, one of whom we should
expect it least, George Wharton James,[8] misstated the case
to the detriment of the Franciscans. "President Durán,"
he writes, "took the bold position of informing the governor
in reply to a query, that the government had no claim whatever upon the hospitality of unsecularized missions," which
of course is nonsense; nor did Fr. Durán make such a declara-
tion. The hospitality of the early missionaries was praised

[6] *The Missions*, etc., vol. iii, p. 30.
[7] Bancroft, *California*, vol. iii, p. 434.
[8] *In And Out Of The Old Missions*, p. 264.

the world over by every traveler who visited California. If there was any one who had a right to such hospitality, it was the head of the territorial government. It is pleasant to note that in the whole history of California no one had the slightest reason for complaint about the treatment received at the hands of the missionaries whether journeying as a stranger or as an acquaintance.

José M. Ramírez, who as ensign had come to California with Echeandia in 1825, appeared at Santa Inés in July, 1836, to receive as commissioner the Mission with all its belongings. He seems to have at once turned over the property to José M. Covarrúbias, who had been appointed administrator. At all events, the inventory drawn up was signed on August 1st by Fr. José Joaquin Jimeno and José M. Covarrúbias, and with that the Mission was confiscated and in control of a government agent. The inventory ran as follows:

Credits, or what was due the Mission....	$ 1,892.87
Buildings of the Mission..............	945.00
Furniture, implements, and contents of storeroom........................	14,527.63
Cattle, 8,040 head...................	24,850.00
Sheep, 1,923 head....................	1,469.00
Horses, 343 head.....................	886.00
Mules, 45 head......................	540.00
Orchard with 987 fruit trees...........	987.00
Church building......................	4,000.00
Church goods, sacred vessels, etc........	6,251.62
Library of the Fathers, sixty-six volumes.	188.50
Total Valuation....................	$56,437.62
Debts of the Mission..............	5,475.00
	$50,962.62

In this document the church edifice is described as "a nave 43¾ varas, or about 124 feet long, and 9 varas or 25 feet wide, inside measure; the walls of adobe with four doors and 8 windows with glass panes; a room which serves as vestry, 9 varas long and 6 varas wide, having three doors and one window, and a floor of burnt brick. The whole building, church and vestry, is roofed with tiles. The ceiling of the church is of boards, and the floor of brick."[9]

The appointment of Covarrúbias meant trouble for the missionaries. He belonged to the clique of Pio Pico whose aim was to wipe out the Missions everywhere. Covarrúbias had married a niece of Pio Pico, and could be depended upon to carry out Pico's wishes.

VIEW OF CONSTRUCTION OF THE WATER WORKS SYSTEM, ALL OF SOLID MASONRY.

Soon after taking over the temporal management of Santa Inés Mission, the administrator had a dispute with Fr. José Joaquin Jimeno about the use of the coutryard, where he wanted his cattle and horses to roam at will. By law the clergy was allowed one-half of the buildings fronting on the courtyard or patio, and the use of that much of the yard nearest the church. The other half was granted to Covarrúbias and family. Fr. Jimeno had a cow or two, and likewise a horse or two. An ugly scene occurred, which we dare not describe,

[9] *Cal. Arch., St. Pap., Missions* vol. vi, pp. 27-28. Bancroft Collection.

because the description rests on the testimony of the Indians almost entirely and is anything but flattering to the administrator. Fernandito is our authority, who had the facts from the Indians when he arrived nearly twenty years later. In order to prevent any further trouble, Fr. Jimeno had some Indians build a wall between the portion used by the Fathers and the part claimed by Covarrúbias. This wall was built of large boulders laid in adobe mortar, and ran through the property to its limits nearly 300 feet distant. Tiles capped the wall to protect it against the rains.

Covarrúbias served as administrator from July, 1836, to February 6, 1837, when another inventory was drawn up and the property turned over to Francisco Cota. This inventory signed by Covarrúbias and Cota on January 27, 1837, values the Mission property at $44,772, and notes the debts as amounting to $5,487.

The neophyte population was given as consisting of 335 souls. Two years later, February, 1839, the list still contained the names of 315 Indians. Cota complained, however, that the working animals had dwindled to 80 horses and 30 mules.[10]

On December 31, 1838, Cota drew up another inventory. This shows that the debts had been reduced. He gave the total value of the property in his charge as $47,362.12, and the debts as $2,713.37, leaving the unencumbered assets of $44,648.75.[11]

On January 1, 1839, the monthly salaries were as follows:

Missionary in charge, Fr. José Joaquin Jimeno	$83.34
The Very Rev. Fr. Prefecto Narciso Durán	41.65
Divine Worship	41.65
Secretary Ramon Malo	25.00
Administrator, Francisco Cota	50.00
First mayordomo, Joaquin Villa	15.00
Second mayordome, Miguel Valencia	12.00

---

[10] *Cal. Arch., St. Pap., Missions* vol. vi, p. 31. Bancroft Collection.
[11] *Cal. Arch., St. Pap., Missions* vol. vi, pp. 29-30. Bancroft Collection.

Keeper of the keys or watchman, José
    Linares............................... 10.00
Servant, Francisco Guilbet?................ 10.00
_____
$288.64[12]

On January 19, 1839, Governor J. B. Alvarado appointed an inspector for the California Missions in the person of William Hartnell, who began his investigations at San Diego on May 22nd. He reached Santa Inés early in July. What he saw was discouraging. He discovered for one thing that there were not enough Indians to brand the cattle. Most of the neophytes had run away. Those who by reasons of age, infirmity, or attachment to the missionaries, remained, had not received any clothing for the last two years. The working horses and mules had already been so reduced by having to supply the needs of the troops at Santa Barbara that in 1837, as the administrator complained, only eighty horses and thirty mules still belonged to the Mission. Hartnell ordered Administrator Francisco Cota to slaughter 300 cattle for the purpose of purchasing, with the hides and tallow, $1,000 worth of clothing which he was to distribute to the neophytes.[13]

In virtue of Alvarado's Reglamento of March 1st, 1840, Fr. José J. Jimeno on October 17, 1840, proposed Miguel Cordero for mayordomo of Mission Santa Inés. Governor Alvarado approved the choice and made the appointment on October 23rd.[14] According to Bancroft, the inventory compiled at the time showed a valuation, exclusive of lands and church property, of $49,115, against which stood a debt of only $975. Buildings, implements, and contents of the storerooms, $12,287; live stock, consisting of 10,295 cattle, 1,704 sheep, 525 horses, 32 mules, and 49 pigs, $34,086; 987 fruit trees, $987; and credits, $1,828. The cattle, as will be seen, reached the highest number in 1841, which was due mainly

[12] *Cal. Arch., St. Pap., Missions*, vol. vi, p. 32.
[13] *Cal. Arch., St. Pap.*, vol. xi, p. 448.
[14] *Archbishop Archives*, No. 2251.

to the excellent pasturage. Sheep had not thrived so well, perhaps owing to the ravages of wild beasts. Withal Cordero seems to have merited the confidence placed in him by Fr. Jimeno. In the same year Cordero was ordered to kill 500 fat cattle on government account, and in the next year an order came from the government of Alvarado to deliver 300 head of cattle to Eulogio Celis. From the experience of other Missions there was no compensation to be expected from this transaction.[15]

The French traveller Eugene Mofras seems to have visited Mission Santa Inés in the month of April, 1842. At all events he writes: "The Mission of Santa Inés lies twelve leagues northwest from the Mission of Santa Barbara, eight leagues from the Mission of Purisima Concepcion, and fifteen leagues south of Mission San Luis Obispo. After one has clambered to the ridge of the sierra, one's eye surveys the east slope, and sees below, towards the center of an extensive prairie, the Mission. It is sheltered from the winds that blow from the sea and from such as blow from the northeast by two parallel ranges. The low flats are irrigated and very productive; the rising grounds are crowned by stately standing timber. Owing to its favorable location, this Mission reached a high degree of wealth during the thirty years from its founding; for in 1834 it had 1,300 Indians, 14,000 head of cattle, 1,200 horses, and 12,000 sheep, and harvested 3,500 fanegas of grain." Here, as at other Missions, Mofras greatly exaggerates the figures. Santa Inés never had more than 720 Indians, and that was in 1817. Likewise all other figures are exaggerated, as the reader will find by comparing the tabular reports in a later chapter. "At the present time," Mofras continues, "owing to the care of the Spanish Father, Fr. Juan Moreno, and his associate, Fr. José Jimeno, the Mission succeeded in keeping 10,000 head of cattle, 500 horses, and 4,000 sheep; but there are in the vicinity no more than 250 Indians. In all California, this Mission is at present the one best provided

---

[15] Bancroft, *California*, vol. iv, Note 27, p. 646.

with horned cattle; but it is to be feared that the government and its agents may soon cause this last trace of wealth to disappear."[16] The two orders for cattle from Governor Alvarado offered good reasons for such fear.

In January, 1842, Alvarado ordered $80 to be expended for church purposes, but of course the money was not to be expected to come from the government. In May the music teacher Luis was ordered to place himself at the disposal of Fr. José Jimeno.[17]

---

[16] Mofras, *Exploration*, vol. i, p. 320; vol. ii, pp. 377-378.
[17] *Cal. Arch., Dep. Records*, vol. xii, p. 165.

CHAPTER V.

On August 25, 1842, Governor Manuel Micheltorena arrived at San Diego from Mexico. He had instructions from the General Government to restore the Missions to the management of the Franciscans. Accordingly, on March 29, 1843, he issued a decree from Los Angeles to that effect.

On April 3rd, Micheltorena addressed the following order to the administrators in charge of Missions: "Pursuant to the decree issued by this superior departmental government under date of March 29th, last past, which you will have seen published, and in conformity to what is literally ordained therein, you will please deliver the Mission in your charge, after the respective inventories have been made, to the Rev. Father whom it may please the Rev. Fr. Presidente to designate, and who may present the order to that effect. You will render an account to this government along with the documents of the transfer and reception in which are specified the buildings, gardens, chattels, farm implements, etc., and will receive the allowance for the time during which you have discharged the office of administrator. God and Liberty. Los Angeles, April 3, 1843."[1] The transfer of Mission Santa Inés was made, but no details nor inventory are extant.

A notable honor was conferred on Mission Santa Inés early in 1844, which distinguishes this establishment from any other Mission in California. The first Bishop appointed for California in 1840, the Rt. Rev. Francisco Garcia Diego, O. F. M., arrived at Santa Barbara in January, 1842, and made the Mission there his residence. He had brought along some students for the priesthood, who were likewise quartered at

---

[1] *The Missions and Missionaries*, vol. iv, pp. 272-277.

the Mission and continued their studies there. The Bishop ere long found that the apartments assigned to him and his ecclesiastical family were unsuitable for a seminary which he

GOVERNOR JOSÉ MANUEL MICHELTORENA

desired to establish on a larger scale. At best, too, the Bishop, the professors, and students were but guests, especially before the Mission had been restored to the Fathers. Early in 1844, therefore, he instructed Fathers J. J. Jimeno, and Juan Moreno of Santa Inés, and Fr. Francisco Sanchez of his little seminary, to petition Governor Micheltorena for a grant of land within the territory of Mission Santa Inés for the purpose of establishing and maintaining a seminary there. The Governor readily acceded to the request, and on March 16, 1844, wrote to the three Fathers as follows: "To Fathers J. J. Jimeno, Francisco Sanchez, and Juan Moreno. I have the honor of transmitting to Your Reverences the Title to land which you solicited for a college seminary to be established at Santa Inés. In addition I will deliver annually $500 in silver to whomsoever Your Reverences may empower, beginning with the current year, on condition that there should be admitted therein, under rules that may be adopted, every inhabitant of the Department, who having been instructed in the rudiments, desires to advance in higher studies."[2] On the same date the governor sent a similar note to the Bishop.

Under date of March 27, 1844, the three Fathers replied: "We have received the title which Your Excellency deigned to transmit to us, and at the same time we have received the official note which accompanies it. We cheerfully accept the $500 which the liberality of Your Excellency annually pays for the College Seminary; but we should like that this amount be for establishing some scholarships; for we think of securing others according to the capacity of the seminary funds. However, others will have to agree to pay the amount annually which the Statutes formulated by the Bishop may assign for those of whom we shall take charge in obedience to Your Excellency.

"Although into the College Seminary only such ought to be admitted as have already been instructed in the first rudiments; yet, as in this country that may be an obstacle to its rapid growth, we have determined to establish a primary school for which we expect Your Excellency's protection

---

[2] *California Archives, Dep. Records*, vol, xiii, pp. 134-135.

and counsels. We have the honor, etc., Santa Inés, March 27, 1844. Fr. José Joaquin Jimeno, Fr. Juan Moreno, Fr. Francisco Sanchez."[3]

The Bishop himself acknowledged his obligations as follows: "Most Excellent Sir:—By the official note of Your Excellency of the 16th instant, I have been with pleasure advised not only of the noble sentiments which animate you to appreciate the education of the young, but also of your vivid desires to cooperate, and to protect the establishments that tend to such grand objects. I very much congratulate myself on this, and I accept, in the name of the young Church, the land which at Mission Santa Inés it has pleased Your Excellency to donate for the maintenance of the Seminary, which we contemplate erecting; and I at once give you with my sincere gratitude the most sincere thanksgiving.

"The absolute want of resources in which I find myself, and which renders precarious my own subsistence, has obliged me to approach the piety of my diocesan children so that they with voluntary donations create a fund that may sustain my Seminary. I hope in the goodness of God that He will bless and multiply said fund. Therefore I ordain in the Constitutions which are to govern my Seminary, that a primary school shall be provided in addition to the classes of Latin, etc., and that as many poor boys may there be received and clothed so far as may be possible for said fund. Nevertheless, in accordance with the regular order and usage of every College, I at the same time determine that boys, who may be the sons of wealthy parents, shall pay annually for the expense of boarding, etc., the moderate pension of $350. The generous offer which Your Excellency has the goodness to make to me of $500 annually to be paid in silver at Monterey, I understand is in favor of poor boys only of this Department (territory), who are to be admitted into the Seminary, educated, boarded, and clothed free of charge, but not for the sons of the rich who should pay for their board at least, whilst it is

[3] *Archbishop Archives, No.* 2274   It is clear, therefore, that the three Fathers did not present their petition at Monterey, as is claimed.

MOST REV. BISHOP FRANCISCO GARCIA DIEGO, O. F. M., D. D.

given to all others free of charge. If the obligation which Your Excellency attaches to your donation is granted with this understanding, I accept at once, and give you for it the most cordial thanksgivings. I shall notify the Fr. Rector of my Seminary, the Fr. José Joaquin Jimeno, that he render returns for it punctually. God keep Your Excellency many years. Hospice Episcopal at Santa Barbara, March 27, 1844. Fr. Francisco, Bishop of the Californias."[4]

The governor wrote on the margin of this letter that the Bishop had understood correctly, that the $500 would be paid to the person who presents invoice to that effect.

The lands granted by Governor Micheltorena, six square leagues, embraced the Cañadas of Sotonocmo (Sotonocomú), Alisguey, Calabaza, and Aguichumú. On September 26, 1844, the governor granted two additional pieces of land. In April, 1845, juridical possession was given of the lands, on which occasion it was promised that during the existence of the College one holy Mass each year should be celebrated for the soul of Nicholas Den, the alcalde who gave possession.[5] The Seminary now possessed 35,499 acres of land for its support. This estate was subsequently known as *La Cañada de los Pinos*, or *College Ranch*.

At last the great day dawned on which the happy Bishop could personally and canonically open the Seminary which he had planned even before he landed in the territory. A document commemorating the event was drawn up and signed on the spot. It reads as follows:

ERECTION OF THE COLLEGE OF OUR LADY DE REFUGIO

"On May 4th, 1844, there being assembled in the church of Mission Santa Inés, Virgin and Martyr, on the morning of May 4, 1844, the Rt. Rev. Bishop of this Diocese, Fr. Francisco Garcia Diego y Moreno, with the Rev. Fathers José

[4] *Archbishop Archives*, No. 2276.
[5] Bancroft, *California*, vol. vi, pp. 425-426.

Mission Santa Ines 55

Joaquin Jiméno, Antonio Jiméno, Juan Moreno, and Fran-
cisco de Jesus Sanchez, the priest, Rev. Miguel Gómez, and
the attendants of His Lordship, the Subdeacon Dorotéo
Ambrís and Gervásio Valadéz, together with the Collegians
José de los Santos Ávila, Alejo Salmon Agapíto Cabrera,
Ramon Gonzales, Diego Villa, and the undersigned Secretary,
for the purpose of celebrating the solemn erection which His
Lordship determined upon of the Conciliar Seminary of this
Diocese on this day already named. After his Lordship had
celebrated the Pontifical Mass in honor of the Most Holy
Virgin de Refugio, he · pronounced a discourse appropriate
to the object of the celebration, and then commanded the
undersigned to read the Constitutions which in the future are
to govern in the Seminary. This reading having been concluded, His Lordship declared that, in accordance with the
Holy Council of Trent, the Seminary of the Diocese was established, and in virtue of the same it could thereafter enjoy all
the honors, rights, and privileges, which according to (Canon)
law are granted to the Seminaries of Catholic Dioceses. After
this His Lordship bestowed his solemn benediction upon the
whole people assembled in the same church for the great
function; and, I the undersigned, by order of His Lordship,
drew up the present *Acta*, which His Lordship signed together
with the rest of the persons already mentioned, and to which
I, the undersigned Secretary of the Diocese, bear testimony
on the same date etc., as above.—Fr. Francisco, Bishop of
the Californias, Fr. José Joaquin Jimeno, Rector, Fr. Francisco de Jesus Sanchez, Vice-Rector, Fr. Juan Moreno, Professor of Letters, Fr. Antonio Jimeno, José Miguel Gómez,
Priest, Doroteo Ambris, Collegian, Gervasio Valladez, Collegian, José de los Santos Ávila, Collegian, Alejo Salmon,
Collegian, Agapíto Cabrera, Collegian, Ramon Gonzales,
Collegian, Diego Villa. To which I testify, Fr. José Maria
de Jesus Gonzales Rúbio, Secretary."

The Constitutions written by Fr. Gonzales, exclusive of
the title page, cover fifteen pages, the size of ordinary type-
writer paper. The signature of the Bishop and that of his

secretary, Fr. Gonzales Rubio, are on page 16. In the left-hand corner below is the seal of the Bishop, of which a fac-simile accompanies this paper.

About a year and half later, October 21, 1845, the Rector, Fr. José J. Jimeno, could report to the Bishop that thirty-five boys were then studying at the seminary. This pleased Bishop Diego very much. In turn he blessed the Fathers for the great work they were doing under peculiar difficulties.[6]

With regard to the building of the ecclesiastical seminary, (not to be confounded with the later College erected a mile and a half from the Mission) we found that it was built by Fr. José Jimeno in the courtyard about fifty feet farther back of the vestry westward, and fitted in between the south line of the church and the dividing wall raised by Fr. Jimeno to avoid having trouble with the mayordomos, hence a distance of 118 or 120 feet. It was sixty feet wide including the cor-ridor facing the front wing. The walls consisted of adobes and the structure had two stories. The second floor facing the front wing had also a porch or corridor. The lower floor was divided into class rooms, and rooms for the professors. The upper floor contained the dormitories. The roof was covered with tiles.

The dining room was where former priests had it, in the rear of the front wing. The kitchen of adobes stood a few yards from the dining room in the courtyard.

The choir for chanting the Divine Office was in the gallery at the rear of the church. Access to it was by means of a stairs that ran along the church wall from the inner court-yard. The singing was entirely Gregorian.[7]

The space from the rear of the seminary to the limits of the lot was used for the cows and horses belonging to the ecclesiastical community.

---

[6] *Libro Borrador*, Santa Barbara; *Archbishop's Archives*, San Francisco.

[7] For regulations of the Church on Liturgical Music, see our volume on *Mission San Juan Bautista*, Appendix F. What is said there applies more emphatically at Santa Inés, because the choir here was composed of Ecclesiastics and Collegians.

As already stated, Mission Santa Inés, by decree of Governor Manuel Micheltorena, dated March 29, 1843, was restored to the management of the Franciscans. On March 18, 1844, Fr. Comisario Prefecto Narciso Durán reported to the Mexican Government on Mission Santa Inés: "It has been kept in a tolerably good condition. Means to support the Indian neophytes are not lacking. The spiritual and temporal administration is in the hands of Fr. José Joaquin Jimeno. The number of neophytes is 264."[8]

SEAL OF THE MOST REV. BISHOP FRANCISCO GARCIA DIEGO, O. F. M., D. D.

Alas! Governor Micheltorena for his fairness to the Missions suffered the fate of the noble Governor Manuel Victoria, and for the same reason. The paisano chiefs never forgave him for taking the management of the Missions and of the neophytes out of the selfish hands of the unscrupulous clique headed by Juan B. Alvarado and Pio Pico. They resolved to force him out of the territory, knowing full well that the Mexican Government was unable to punish them. The kindly Micheltorena was accordingly compelled to leave California

---

[8] *The Missions and Missionaries*, vol. iv, pp. 322-323; 325-333.

in March, 1845. This action, of course, also deprived the seminary of the contribution annually received from the governor.

Immediately the paisano chiefs in accord with their leader planned to obtain control of the Mission property and of the labor of the Indians. Micheltorena, in agreement with the Mexican Government, had declared that the property of the neophytes at the Missions was as much private property as that of the white settlers. Under Spanish law such holdings could not be taken from the Indians without their consent. The paisano chief, however, insisted that it was government property, and under this head he sought a pretext. He claimed the missionaries disposed of mission property without a permit. Fr. Durán in a Circular informed the Fathers of the accusation. For Mission Santa Inés, Fr. Jimeno answered the accusers in this fashion: "I have read the Circular," he writes to Fr. Durán on April 26, 1845, "and shall do what it commands. At the same time, I cannot help making known the pain which it caused me to see that we are all harassed for offences which we have not committed. Let them point out the one who made the sale, and what indispensable utensils were sold; and let such a one vindicate himself, or, if he cannot, let him be reprimanded; but without proving that which they impute to us, and even without examining the matter, to call such charge just, as Your Paternity does, and for you to say that the two letters are written with moderation and justice, makes it most painful to any heart, and more so to the heart of men who in truth should not be so badly requited. It is a notorious fact that calumnies are spread with impunity, and that pretexts are sought in order to show that the interests of the Indians are not safe in our hands, and that it is necessary that others manage them. Notwithstanding this, to believe and to take for granted what has not been proved, is an outrage against whomsoever is treated in this manner."

Three weeks later, May 13, 1845, Fr. José Jimeno reported that the assets of the Mission consisted of thirty-five hides and 350 lbs. of tallow. The Mission owed to various parties

$1,608. "In the past year, with the approval of the governor, the number of cattle was reduced. The laborers were promised their wages in cattle, but, in the end, drafts had to be given them, because the horses were crippled and the cattle lean, whilst the families of these serving were large and in urgent need."[9]

Pico, however, had determined to do away with the Missions, as he himself confesses in his *Narracion Historica.* "The principal object which guided me," he writes, "in my actions respecting those establishments, was to make the rule of the Missions disappear completely." Accordingly, he had his subservient assembly declare that the Missions should be leased and finally sold. Commissioners were appointed to take over estates, to begin with. Those appointed for the transaction at Santa Inés were Pico's brother Andres Pico and Juan Manso. They drew up an *Inventorio* on July 28th, but it was done in such a slipshod manner that Fr. J. Jimeno wrote to Governor Pio Pico under date of July 29, 1845: "The comisionados for the Missions have concluded here as they saw fit. What they have put into the inventory, or what they left out to be put in, I do not know; for in this matter I played no greater part than did the lowest Indian. I have never seen anything more exotic and strange in the way of making inventories, and in ceding and receiving property; for I, who surrendered it, had neither any share in it, nor any knowledge of many things done, nor does my signature appear on the inventory. Hence the transaction is null and void. About many things neither he who received the property, nor the comisionados themselves, had any information. There may be various reasons for this precipitous proceeding, about which I should say nothing save that I protest against the *manner* in which the management of the temporalities was taken from me, but not for having taken it at all; for in this they have done me a favor."[10]

[9] *The Missions and Missionaries,* vol. iv, pp. 356-357.
[10] *The Missions and Missionaries,* vol. iv, p. 388.

The inventory compiled by Andrés Pico and Juan Manso reported the following valuation as appraised by them: Buildings, implements, and effects in the storehouse, $7,943; lands, gardens, 692 fruit trees, five sites of grazing land, $5,240; live stock 496 head of cattle, besides 965 head due from seven private individuals, 1,608 sheep, 193 horses, 18 mules, and 33 pigs, $5,093; credits $1,736. Total valuation, $20,288. The debits amounted to $2,848, not enough to justify the false claim of Pico that he had to rent and even sell the Mission to satisfy creditors.[11]

Andres Pico and Juan Manso jointly on July 28, 1845, wrote to the governor's secretary from Santa Inés that Fr. Narciso Durán, on July 22, 1845, had told them that whatever was due him from the Missions of Santa Inés and San Buenaventura, he would donate to the neophytes of those same Missions.[12]

Pico's next step was to lease the Mission. This action, too, was illegal, as the General Government had not approved his plan to wipe out the Missions; on the contrary, it *forbade any change to be made in the status of these establishments.* The highest offer of rental came from José M. Covarrúbias and Joaquin Carrillo, $580 a year. On December 5, 1845, they were accordingly permitted to occupy the buildings and manage the Indians for a term of nine years at a rental of $580 annually.[13]

This amount received from the lessees annually was to be divided into three parts, the neophytes, divine worship, and the missionary. The proceeds from the rent being $580 a year would yield $16 a month to each division. The 255 surviving neophytes would each then receive six and one-half cents a month. This glorious share the now entirely free Indians might increase by laboring for the lessee, or by tilling the little plots of land graciously conceded by Pico out of the

[11] Bancroft, *California*, vol. iv, p. 646, note.
[12] *The Missions and Missionaries*, vol. iv, pp. 454-455.
[13] *Cal. Arch., St. Pap., Missions*, vol. xi, pp. 984-988; *The Missions and Missionaries* pp. 446, 458, 459.

thousands of acres they had cultivated and made productive, but which were now owned by the chief paisanos or their friends. What of the missionaries, however? How were they to live? If one Father resided at the Mission, he would receive $16 a month with which he would have to maintain himself; but at Mission Santa Inés two Fathers attended to the remnant Indians there and at extinct Purisima. So each one received $8 a month. This, as Fr. José Jimeno observed in a letter to Pico, would not pay for the meat. Even this bit of meat they would have to prepare for themselves, unless they could procure the services of some kindly Indian for nothing. Instead of relieving the missionaries, Pico had another plan in his mind, which will be presented in the next chapter.

CHAPTER VI.

The unhappy consequences of Pio Pico's usurpations will
be easily inferred from the two letters reproduced here in full.
One was addressed to Pico on January 21, 1846, by Fr. José
Joaquín Jimeno, who wrote: "My esteemed Señor: Persuaded
that Your Excellency must be penetrated with reason and
justice, and at the same time impelled by necessity, I have
determined to direct this letter to you in order to make manifest to you our sad condition. When the comisionados placed
here a mayordomo, I asked him in what state would be divine
worship and its ministers. He replied that he had no orders
to give anything, and that he would have to provide only the
board that he was obliged to offer. These were the instructions which he had. This answer, made repeatedly, did not
fail to cause me some pain; but as I believed that the plan of
renting the Mission would be quickly effected, it seemed to
me expedient to suffer for this short time. It has been put off
now these six months, however, during which space we adapted
ourselves by securing besides bread, meat, and some tallow
drippings, and candles, a little flour for the kitchen, all through
some hardship. After this misery we find ourselves in another,
to which we are subjected by the third part of the scant rental
of the Mission, which being $16 a month, eight for divine
worship and eight for the missionary, does not suffice to pay
for the meat. In view of this, I supplicate Your Excellency
to be pleased to make of the proceeds from the rent only two
parts (instead of three), one for divine worship and for the
missionary, and one for the Indians. Fr. José Joaquin
Jimeno."[1]

---

[1] *California Archives, Dept. St. Pap.* vol. vi, pp. 358-359.

If the reader bears in mind that this Mission, like others in California, was reared and the lands cultivated by the convert Indians under the tutelage of the missionary Fathers for the spiritual and temporal benefit of those same neophytes; and that all was accomplished without any aid,from the governments, least of all from the California governments, he will appreciate the predicament in which the real owners and their spiritual guides now found themselves.

The other letter, likewise addressed to Pio Pico, but by Jouaquin Carrillo, the lessee of Mission Santa Inés, is also very enlightening. "My Esteemed Uncle and Señor," Carrillo writes. "By means of the inventories which Señor Cordero sends to your office you will be informed of the state in which

this Mission is. From them you will infer the little there is for advancing it. The orchard produces nothing else than apples, as it is very much ruined. There is sufficient land for cultivation, but planting cannot be done on a large scale because the water with which it must be irrigated comes through the land of another owner. There are no cattle, and the sheep are few. Hence I am not a little hard up. In addition to all this the Father (Fr. J. J. Jimeno) takes no part in the renting for reasons sufficiently weighty, which he has explained to me. However, I have not for all that ceased to discover means so that the lease may not be burdensome to me, bearing in mind that the establishment cannot produce anything more.

"The said Father has proposed to me to solicit from the government that the $580 rental of each year be divided into two parts, one for divine worship and the other for the Indians." Carrillo then recommends that the proposition be accepted. The Father had also asked that the rent due should be paid every three months, instead of at the close of a year, as that would also be easier for the lessee. He left it to Pico to decide. Carrillo then goes on to tell the governor that "the Indians have presented themselves to me, and have delivered a memorial which they wished me to transmit to the government, and which I enclose. It gives you all the information. It seems to me well to recommend it to you in order that it be treated with consideration. In this way perhaps it may be prevented that the Indians disperse and go to work. I am not very much pleased that therein they ask for six yoke of oxen, although they may oblige me to give them from those not yet trained to the yoke."[2]

Pio Pico had no intention to preserve the Missions. He wanted to wipe them out, as he himself declared. Moreover, he was in a hurry about it, lest the Mexican Government might interfere. His plan must have leaked out, even before Carrillo's letter reached Los Angeles, Pico's capital; for the Fr. Comisario Prefecto, under date of January 26, 1846, from Santa Barbara, wrote to Pico: "For some days it has been rumored around here that it is contemplated to sell Mission Santa Inés in order to pay the debts it has contracted with merchant ships. This, if true, seems to me a very bold step. It would be expedient to see first whether the debts could not be paid with the cattle which the Mission still possesses; for, inasmuch as that Mission has not been abandoned by its neophytes, it seems to me that it ought not to be treated like those that are abandoned. I believe that this merits the consideration of Your Excellency, and that you will condescend that this step be taken.—Fr. Narciso Durán."[3]

[2] *California Archives, Departmental St. Pap.*, vol. vii, pp. 364-366.
[3] *Archbishop Archives*, No. 2334.

Pico replied under date of February 6, 1846: "I do not know why it may have been said that the government thought of selling Mission Santa Inés; for this is a matter which I never contemplated, (?) notwithstanding that some difficulties arose with regard to paying the debts, difficulties which have been surmounted by the lessees themselves, who have bound themselves to pay them on condition that the branded cattle remain in their charge for the benefit as well as the assets or claims of the Mission."[4]

On February 11, 1846, Fr Durán then wrote a long letter to Pico in which this passage occurs: "I am satisfied with what Your Excellency says regarding Santa Inés. What grieves me is the scantiness of the allowance assigned, and I do not know how they will escape dying of hunger. Yet, *the two religious are a great credit to the ministry.* Would that some means might be found to improve their condition."[5]

This was Fr. Durán's last communication to Pico, at least the last one extant. He had persistently exposed the iniquity of which Pico was guilty against the property of the neophytes and Pico had therefore always sought some shadow of legality. From that time the governor had his own way entirely. He accordingly hastened the work of wiping out the Missions, very likely for the reason that during the months of February or March an order came from the General Government of Mexico forbidding any change in the status of the Missions. He suppressed the document, and continued with the sale of what was neither his property nor that of the California government, but the property of the neophytes. He wanted the money, however, for his own schemes. The reader will find

---

[4] *The Missions and Missionaries*, vol. iv, pp. 467-467.
[5] *The Missions and Missionaries*, vol. iv, p. 469.

the exposure of the whole sordid transaction in volumes iii and iv of *The Missions and Missionaries*. Finally, although Mission Santa Inés, because it was devoted to the education of seminarians, had been exempted from sale by the assembly in August, 1844; and although Pico himself declared in January 1846 that he had not thought of selling the Mission, on June 15, 1846, Mission Santa Inés was sold to José M. Covarrúbias, and Joaquin Carrillo for $7,000. Pio Pico had triumphed. The title deed, or *Escritura de Venta*, is not extant. It read probably like the one for Mission San Buenaventura, which laid down certain conditions for the observance of the purchasers. One of these obliged the purchasers to furnish whatever was necessary for the subsistence and clothing of the ministering priest, and for the continuance of divine worship, and to set aside the apartments which the priest then occupied for his habitation.[6]

Only three weeks later, July 7, 1846, the United States flag was raised at Monterey. With that move paisano misrule ceased, and respect for Church and Indian property became the rule. Nay, even the property sold over the heads of the clergy in charge was later restored to the church; but that is another story to be related in the next chapter.

We know little of what occurred at Mission Santa Inés regarding temporal affairs. Bancroft notes that Joaquin Carrillo, Agustin Janssens, Francisco Cota, and José M. Covarrúbias were named justices of the peace of the so-called pueblo. On September 6, 1847, by order of Colonel R. B. Mason, military Governor of California, Secretary of State, H. W. Halleck, wrote to the lessees, José M. Covarrúbias and Joaquin Carrillo—"Sirs: In order to enable him to act understandingly upon matters connected with the Mission of Santa Inés, the Governor directs that the renters of that Mission immediately furnish him with copies of the contract, or agreement, by which they occupy said Mission, and also a full account of all rents paid, with the proper receipts for the same. Very etc., H. W. Halleck, Lt. of Engineers, and Secre-

[6] *The Missions and Missionaries*, vol. iv, pp. 509-511.

tary of State."—Covarrúbias and Carrillo were having a taste of the bitter soup Pico had cooked for the Fathers and Indians.

On the same date Halleck sent the following illuminating communication to one Joaquin Aquila of Santa Inés. "Sir: The Governor directs me to acknowledge the receipt of your letter of the 26th August, enclosing certain papers purporting to be a title to a piece of land in or near the Mission of Santa Inés. The title to which you refer is of no value, Captain José Maria Flores having had no proper authority to make such grant; but as you are in possession of said land, you may continue to hold it (provided no other person presents a better claim) until the proper tribunals are organized for the investigation of questions of that character. Your papers are enclosed herewith. Very etc., H. W. Halleck."[7]

Captain Flores mentioned in the letter succeeded to the command of the California forces after the flight of Pio Pico. Neither had Pico any authority to sell the Mission, and the U. S. Court so declared later on. Meanwhile the purchasers of the Mission received a lucid communication from Col. Mason, which foreshadowed what was to come. It read as follows: "Headquarters Tenth Military Department, Monterey, California, November 29, 1847.—Gentlemen: Your communication of the 23rd October is before me. I cannot, with the information with which I am at present possessed, recognize you as the legal purchasers of the Mission of Santa Inés. The authority given by the departmental assembly of April 3, 1846, to sell the Missions, expressly required that they should be sold at *public auction*, the *customary notice* being *previously given*. This was not done: the Mission was not sold at public auction, but, on the contrary, you yourselves say that you entered into a contract with the government by which you became the purchasers; and if you became the purchasers on the 15th of June, 1846, how is it that you continued to pay rent during all that year, and part of 1847?

[7] *California and New Mexico, Execute Document No.* 17, pp. 392, 393.

For this and other reasons, I declare there has been no legal sale, and the obligations under which you stood previous to the 15th of June, 1846, as the renters of said Mission, to be in full force and effect. You will, therefore, without delay, pay up the amount due according to the terms of the contract by which you became the renters of the Mission of Santa Inés, a copy of which contract you will send to this office, as also copies of the receipts for the amount of rent paid since the 1st of January, 1846. You sent a statement of the amount paid, but I wish a copy of the receipt by the Padre Jimeno. I am etc., R. B. Mason."[8]

In explanation it must be noted here that Secretary Halleck, under date of August 23, 1847, had inquired of the Administrator of the vacant Diocese, the Very Rev. Fr. José Gonzales Rubio, as to the sale of Mission Santa Inés, the rent paid previously, and the securities the purchasers gave to the government. In a long letter Fr. Gonzales replied under date of September 14, 1847, that he had no such documents; that they must be in the archives of the former government, and with the purchasers Carrillo and Covarrúbias. On November 18, 1847, Fr. Gonzales referred to the former letter to which he had received no answer, and then again pleaded that the occupants of the Mission property be made to pay the rent which they had neglected to do. He notes that the rental was $580 a year, half of which went to the neophytes and the other half to the Fathers for their maintenance, for divine worship, and for the sustenance of the students in the seminary.[9]

Fr. José Joaquin and Fr. Francisco Sanchez, as rector and vice-rector respectively continued in charge of the College Seminary. According to Bancroft,[10] they reported the financial condition on December 31, 1848, as follows: Receipts

[8] *Executive Document No.* 17, p. 436.—"Though they kept possession until after 1848 under their lease, their title by purchase was finally declared invalid."—Bancroft, vol. v, p.635.

[9] *Libro Borrador.*

[10] Bancroft, *California*, vol. v, p. 635.

MISSION SANTA INES BEFORE EARTHQUAKE.

from parents of pupils, $58; from sales of live stock, $667; from the Bishop, $250; from the rector, $239; from the vice-rector, $300; from American friends, $25; from alms, $96. Total receipts, $1,635.—Expenditures, $1,846. Deficit of 1848, $211; deficit of 1847, $337. Grain harvested in 1848, only 226 fanegas. Cattle belonging to the institution at end of 1848,—1,706 head. This shows that the rental from the Mission property was urgently needed, as Fr. Gonzales wrote to Halleck. It will be seen, too, that the two Fathers, Jimeno and Sanchez, were putting all their personal earnings into the Seminary, a practice which the Franciscans had observed in the case of the Missions. They retained nothing for themselves.

An item of interest is that the Very Rev. Administrator of the Diocese, Fr. Gonzales Rubio, on September 5, 1848, gave Fr. José J. Jimeno permission to build a public chapel at the point called "San Isidoro in the jurisdiction of Santa Inés, so that the people in the vicinity might be enabled to assist at holy Mass, inasmuch as the Father in charge and the students reside there most frequently."

Bishop Garcia Diego, writing to the Fathers at Santa Inés under date of April 16, 1844, informed them that, according to the Council of Trent, Session 22, and according to the present discipline, he could not permit the celebrating of holy Mass in a private chapel; and that therefore, as no reason had been presented why the chapel at the Rancho del Seminario should be considered a public oratory, he could not give the permission asked for.[11] Since then, it seems, settlers and servants attended divine services in said chapel, and so it had actually become a chapel for the public, which accounts for the granting of the permit.

Fr. J. J. Jimeno and Fr. Francisco Sanchez continued in charge of the College until May 7, 1850, when they surrendered the management of the institution to the Revds. Theodosius Bousseier and Felix Migorel of the Congregation of the

---

[11] *Libro de Gobierno*, Los Angeles.

Sacred Hearts of Jesus and Mary. They had arrived at San Francisco from Valparaiso, Chili, in March, and had received the usual faculties from Father Gonzales Rubio, the Administrator, on May 2nd. Thereupon they proceeded to Santa Inés. For their maintenance, and for the support of the College, the extensive farm and the live stock were transferred to their management on condition that, in obedience to the regulations of the Council of Trent, they rendered an exact account to the Ordinary of the Diocese. At the same time both Fathers were to attend the Missions of Santa Inés and Purisima.[12]

After Fathers Jimeno and Sanchez had withdrawn to Mission Santa Barbara, in acknowledgment of their past services Father Gonzales Rubio, the Administrator of the Diocese, accorded them the following well-deserved praises:

"By the official note of Your Reverences, dated April 29th, last past, I am advised of your voluntary resignation of the direction and administration of the Seminary of this diocese, which from its foundation down to the present day you have so worthily had in your care, which resignation I accept with deep regret, merely to please you and to relieve you of the heavy charge.

"From the piety and noble sentiments that characterize Your Reverences, I am convinced that for the assiduous and important labors which you have undergone for the founding and advancement of that Seminary, you have had no other end in view, expected no other recompense, than that which is inseparable from every one who toils for the good. Sublime recompense! and the only one that can satisfy generous souls whom God destines for grand undertakings of public benefit. This reward is to be paid by God, our Lord Whom Your Reverences have served and Who, I am certain, will reward you and crown you far above what is merited.

"However, this confidence in nowise lessens the grati-

[12] *Libro Borrador*, Santa Barbara Mission.

tude which I as Administrator of the diocese owe you; but, inasmuch as the noble generosity of Your Reverences on the one hand, the poverty and uselessness of my person on the other, embarrass me how to recompense you as you deserve, be pleased, Your Reverences, to accept at least the sincere homage of my gratitude, and the cordial thanks which I render you, as well in my name as in the name of this whole Diocese. While I live I shall offer my prayers to the Lord on high that forever in heaven may shine, and on this earth may never be forgotten, the distinguished names of the Rev. Fathers, the Founders of the Seminary of Our Lady of Guadalupe in California.

"On this same date there will be named to succeed Your Reverences, the Rev. Fathers Theodosius Bousseier and Felix Migorel. I hope that, when Your Reverences turn over the church and the seminary in your charge, you will draw up in duplicate a minute inventory, one copy of which you will transmit for the archives of the diocese. May it please Your Reverences, etc.—Fr. José Maria de Jesus Gonzáles, Santa Barbara, May 7th, 1850."[13]

---

[13] *Santa Barbara Archives. Libro Borrador.* So Fathers Jimeno and Sanchez withdrew from Santa Inés as poor as they had gone there.

CHAPTER VII

Property of Mission Santa Inés Returned to the Catholic Church.— Survey
of the Lands.—United States Patent Signed by President Abraham
Lincoln.

From Chapter Sixth the reader will have learned that
Mission Santa Inés was sold to private parties for $7,000.
Only a month later the United States forces raised the Stars
and Stripes over the customhouse at Monterey, and thus put
an end to the machinations of the last governor of Mexican
extraction, the unworthy Pio Pico. After due investigation,
the United States Officials, and the Land Commission organized to examine land claims, declared that Pio Pico's sale of
this and other Missions was illegal, and that what constituted
Church property according to the laws of Spain and Mexico
must revert to the Catholic Church. The Mission lands were
accordingly surveyed by the government surveyor, and then
the United States Patent signed by President Lincoln was
issued to Archbishop José Sadoc Alemany, O. P., Archbishop
of San Francisco, as representative of the Catholic Church.

The document including the survey in detail reads as
follows:

THE UNITED STATES OF AMERICA

"To All To Whom These Presents Shall Come. Greeting:
Whereas it appears from a duly authenticated transcript
filed in the General Land Office of the United States that pursuant to the provisions of the Act of Congress approved the
third day of March, one thousand eight hundred and fifty-one
entitled "An Act to ascertain and settle the Private Land
Claims in the State of California," Joseph Sadoc Alemany,
Roman Catholic Bishop of the Diocese of Monterey, in the
State of California, as claimant, filed his petition on the 19th
day of February, 1853, with the Commissioners to ascertain
and settle the Private Land Claims in the State of California,
sitting as a Board in the City of San Francisco, in which petition he claimed the confirmation to him and his successors of

the title to certain Church property in California, "to be held by him and them in trust for the religious purposes and uses to which the same have been respectively appropriated," said property consisting of "church edifices, houses for the use of the clergy and those employed in the service of the church, church yards, burial grounds, gardens, orchards and vineyards with the necessary buildings thereon and appurtenances," the same having been recognized as the property of said Church by the laws of Mexico in force at the time of the cession of California to the United States, and whereas the Board of Land Commissioners aforesaid on the 18th day of December, 1855, rendered a decree of confirmation in favor of the petitioner for certain lands described therein to be held "in the capacity and for the uses set forth in his petition" the lands at the Mission of Santa Inés, being described in said decree as follows: The Church and the buildings adjoining thereto, erected in the form of a quadrangle, and constituting the Church and Mission buildings of the ancient Mission of Santa Inés, situated in Santa Barbara County, together with the land on which the same are erected, and the curtilage and appurtenances thereunto belonging, and the cemetery as the same is enclosed with its adobe walls, and which adjoin the Church.

"Also a tract of land situated in an easterly direction from said quadrangle at the distance of about eight chains therefrom, known as the Mission Garden, and long occupied by the priests of said Mission with the boundaries as the same is enclosed by fence, and the same as delineated on Map numbered 8 in the Atlas before-mentioned, and there denominated "Orchard and Garden."

"And whereas it further appears from a certified transcript filed in the General Land Office, that an appeal from said decree or decision of the Commissioners having been taken on behalf of the United States to the District Court of the United States for the Southern District of California, and it being shown to the Court that it was not the intention of the United States to prosecute further said appeal, the said District

Court on the 15th of March, 1858, at the regular term "ordered that said appeal be dismissed and said appellee have leave to proceed under the decree of the said Land Commissioners in his favor as a final decree. And whereas, under the 23rd Section of the said Act of March 3rd, 1851, there have been presented to the Commissioner of the General Land Office a plat and certificate of the survey of the tract of land confirmed as aforesaid, authenticated on the 23rd day of October, 1861, by the signature of the Surveyor General of the Public Lands in California, which plat and certificate are in the words and figures following, to wit:

U. S. Surveyor General's Office,
San Francisco, California.

"Under and by virtue of the provisions of the 13th section of the Act of Congress of the 3d of March, 1851, entitled "An Act to ascertain and settle Private Land Claims in the State of California," and of the 12th section of the Act of Congress approved on the 31st of August, 1852, entitled "An Act making Appropriation for the Civil and Diplomatic expenses of the Government for the year ending the 30th of June, 1853, and for other purposes," and in consequence of the annexed copy of a certificate of the United States District Court for the southern District of California having been filed in this Office, whereby it appears that the Attorney General of the United States having given notice that it was not the intention of the United States to prosecute the appeal from the decision of the United States Board of Land Commissioners, said decision having confirmed the title and claim of Joseph Sadoc Alemany, Bishop, etc., to the tract of land designated as the Church and the Mission buildings of the ancient Mission of Santa Inés," the said appeal has been vacated, and thereby the said decision in favor of the said Joseph S. Alemany, has become final. The said tract has been surveyed in conformity with the grant thereof, and the said decision, and I do hereby certify the annexed map to be a true and accurate plat of the said tract of land as appears by the field notes of the survey thereof made by J. E. Terrell, Deputy Surveyor, in the month of October, 1860, under the directions of this office, which having been examined and approved, are now on file therein. And I do further certify that, in accordance with the provisions of the Act of Congress approved on the 14th day of June, 1860, entitled An Act to define and regulate the jurisdiction of the District Court of the United States in California in regard to the survey and location of confirmed private land claims," I have caused to be published once a week for four weeks successively in two newspapers, to wit: The Santa Barbara Gazette, published in the County of Santa Barbara, being the newspaper published nearest to where the said claim is located, the first publication being on the 26th day of September, 1861, and the last on the 17th day of October, 1861. Also in the Southern News, a newspaper published in the City and County of Los Angeles, the first publication being on the 6th day of September, 1861, and the last on the 27th day of September, 1861, a notice that the said claim had been surveyed and a plat made thereof and approved by me. And I do further certify that the said approved plat of survey was retained in this office during all of said four weeks and until the expiration thereof subject to inspection. And I do further certify that no order for the return thereof to the United States District Court has been served upon me. And I do further certify that under and by virtue of the said confirmation, survey, decree, and publication, the said Joseph S. Alemany, Bishop, etc., is entitled to a patent from the United States upon the presentation thereof to the General Land Office for the said tract of Land, the same being bounded and described as follows, to wit:

"Tract of land designated as the Church and Mission buildings and tract No. 1, on the map. Beginning at the ruins at the north east corner of said tract.

"Thence, according to the true meridian, the variation of the magnetic needle being fourteen degrees ten minutes east, north seventy-four degrees west, at forty-four links enters corral and leaves ruins, two chains and ninety-three links to the north-west corner of corral, Station.

"Thence south, sixteen degrees west, at one chain and eighty-nine links leaves corral and enters cemetery, two chains and sixty-nine links to the corner of Church wall, Station.

"Thence along wall of corral, north seventy-four degrees west, two chains and seventy-seven links to the corner of the wall, Station.

"Thence south sixteen degrees west, five chains and thirty links to the south west corner of the wall, Station.

"Thence south, seventy-four degrees east, five chains and thirty links to the south east corner of corral wall, thence along portico five chains and fifty-four links to the corner of the same, Station.

"Thence north, sixteen degrees east, along portico to the north east corner of the same, Station.

"Thence north seventy-four degrees west, along portico twenty-four links to the south east corner of the Church, Station.

"Thence north, sixteen degrees east, at sixty links leaves corner of Church and enters cemetery, one chain to the center of the cemetery, and the south west corner of the ruins, Station.

"Thence, south seventy-four degrees east, thirty-nine links to the south east corner of the ruins, Station, and

"Thence north sixteen degrees east, two chains and thirty links to the point of beginning. Containing three acres and seventy-one hundredths of an acre, and being designated upon the plats of the public surveys, as Lot number thirty-eight, Township Six North Range thirty-one west of the San Bernardino Meridian.

"This tract is connected with the lines of the public surveys as follows, to wit: Beginning at corner number one of said tract and running thence south twelve degrees forty-five minutes west, ninety-four links to Station.

"Thence north fifty-five degrees thirty minutes east, fifty-three chains to an Indian Rancheria, and enters a creek, seventy-five chains to a stone dam across creek, thence along creek at eighty-five chains leave said creek which is forty links wide at this place, course south west, at one hundred

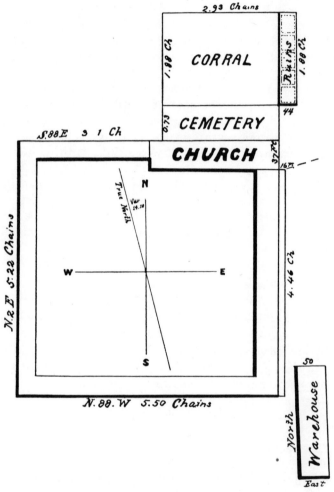

U.S. PATENT RESTORING MISSION PROPERTY TO THE CATHOLIC CHURCH.

and twenty-six chains leaves valley, one hundred and fifty-six chains to Station.

"Thence north thirty-six degrees thirty minutes west, at eleven chains enters valley, twenty chains to Station.

"Thence north five degrees fifteen minutes west, at five chains leaves valley sixty-five chains to Station.

"Thence north three degrees thirty minutes west, at thirty-eight chains crosses road, course south east, fifty-four chains to corner to Sections One, Two, Thirty-Five and Thirty-Six, on line between Township Six and Seven north Range thirty-one west of the San Bernardino Meridian.

"A tract designated as the Warehouse and tract No. II on the map. "Beginning at the north west corner of this tract, from which the south east corner of the portico in tract No. 1 bears south thirty-three degrees thirty minutes west, distant sixty-eight links.

"Thence, according to the true meridian, the variation o f the magnetic needle being fourteen degrees, ten minutes east, along the wall of the Warehouse, south twenty degrees west, two chains and twenty-eight links the south west corner of this tract, Station.

"Thence south seventy degrees east, sixty-five links to the south east corner of this tract, Station.

"Thence north twenty degrees east, two chains and twenty-eight links to the north east corner of this tract, Station, and

"Thence, seventy degrees west, sixty-five links to the point of beginning. Containing fifteen one hundredths of an acre, and being designated upon the plats of the public surveys as Lot number Thirty-Nine, Township Six North, Range Thirty-One west of the San Bernardino Meridian.

"A tract of land designated as ruins of Indian houses and tract No. III on the map. Beginning at the north east corner of the same, from which the south west corner of Tract No. II, bears north forty-seven degrees east, distant thirty-eight links.

"Thence according to the true meridian, the variation of the magnetic needle being fourteen degrees ten minutes east, along the wall of said houses south eight degrees thirty minutes west, four chains and thirty-seven links to the south east corner of this tract, Station.

"Thence north sixty-five degrees thirty minutes west, three chains and sixty-five links to the South west corner of this tract, Station.

"Thence north sixteen degrees east, three chains and eighty-one links to the north west corner of this tract, Station, and

"Thence south seventy-four degrees east, three chains and three links to the point of beginning. Containing one acre, and thirty-four one hundredths of an acre, and being designated upon the plats of the public Surveys as Lot number Forty, Township Six North Range Thirty-One West of the San Bernardino Meridian.

"A tract of land designated as the Water Reservoir and tract No. IV on the map. Beginning at the north west corner of the same from which the south east corner of the ruins in tract No. I, bears north twenty-eight degrees thirty minutes west, distant one chain and forty-nine links.

"Thence, according to the true meridian, the variation of the magnetic needle being fourteen degrees ten minutes east, south thirty-one degrees west, forty-eight links to the south west corner of this tract, Station.

"Thence south fifty-nine degrees east, ninety-six links to the south east corner of this tract, Station.

"Thence north thirty-one degrees east, fifty-nine links to the north east corner of this tract, Station.

"Thence fifty-nine degrees west, sixty-three links to a corner of this tract, Station.

"Thence south thirty-one degrees west, eleven links to a corner of this tract, Station, and

"Thence north fifty-nine degrees west, thirty-three links to the point of beginning. Containing five one hundredths of an acre, and being designated upon the plats of the public surveys as Lot number forty-one, Township Six North Range thirty-one, west of the San Bernardino Meridian.

"A tract of land designated as The Mission Orchard and tract No. V on the map. Beginning at a corner of the same from which the south east corner of the Church in tract No. I bears south and eighty-seven degrees fifteen minutes west, distant eight chains and forty-eight links.

"Thence according to the true meridian, the variation of the magnetic needle being fourteen degrees ten minutes east, south seventy-eight degrees thirty minutes east, six chains and seventy-six links to a corner of this tract, Station.

"Thence south fifteen degrees west, twelve chains and sixty-six links to a corner of this tract, Station.

Thence south eighty-three degrees forty-five minutes west, seven chains and sixteen links to a corner of this tract, Station.

"Thence north twenty-one degrees west, six chains and sixty-three links to a corner of this tract, Station.

"Thence north thirty degrees east, five chains to a corner of this tract, Station, and

"Thence north forty-five degrees fifteen minutes east, four chains and ninety-seven links to the point of beginning. Containing twelve acres and eleven one hundredths of an acre, and being designated upon the plats of the public surveys as Lot number forty-two, Township Six North Range thirty-one west of the San Bernardino Meridian.

SEAL   "In witness whereof I have hereunto signed my "name officially, and caused the seal of my office to be attached at the City of San Francisco, this "23d day of October, A. D. 1861.

"E. F. Beale, U. S. Surveyor General."

"And whereas there has been deposited in the General Land Office of the United States a certificate dated June 27th, 1863, from the Clerk of the United States District Court for the Southern District of California showing that, in the cause entitled J. S. Alemany et al Apellees ads. The United States Appellants, due notice by publication in manner and form as required by law has been made by Surveyor General of the

United States for California in the matter of the approved survey of the Mission Santa Inés confirmed to the claimant and appellee in the above titled cause of J. S. Alemany vs. The United States and that the full period of six months from and after the completion of said publication has elapsed and no objection thereto having been made or filed, the said approved survey has become final and the claimant and appellee entitled to a Patent for the said Mission."

NOW KNOW YE, That the United States of America, in consideration of the premises, and pursuant to the provision of the Act of Congress aforesaid of 3d March, 1851, HAVE GIVEN AND GRANTED, and by these presents DO GIVE AND GRANT unto said Joseph S. Alemany, Bishop of Monterey, and to his Successors, in trust for the religious purposes and uses to which the same have been respectively appropriated, the tracts of land embraced and described in the foregoing survey; but with the stipulation that in virtue of the 15th Section of the said Act the confirmation of this said claim and this patent, "shall not affect the interests of third persons."

To Have and To Hold the said tracts of land with the appurtenances and with the stipulation aforesaid, unto the said Joseph S. Alemany, Bishop of Monterey, and to his Successors, in trust for the religious purposes and uses as aforesaid.

In testimony whereof, I, Abraham Lincoln, President of the United States, have caused these letters to be made Patent, and the Seal of the General Land Office to be hereunto affixed.

Given under my hand at the City of Washington, the twenty third day of May, in the year of our Lord one thousand eight hundred and sixty-two, and of the Independence of the United States the Eighty-Sixth.

By the President,

A. Lincoln

By 2. 9. Stoddard, Secretary.

J. N. Granger, Recorder of the General Land Office. Recorded Vol. 4, pages 108-115 inclusive.

ED. JSW.

CHAPTER VIII.

A most important feature of all the Missions in the hands
of the Franciscans from the earliest days of the Missions anywhere in the United States are the Mission Registers. According to the regulations of the College of San Fernando de
Mexico every Mission had to have the following books: 1—
Baptismal Register; 2—Marriage Register; 3—Burial Register; 4—Confirmation Register; 5—Padron or Register of the
Mission Converts under the following heads: Families, Widowers, Widows, Single Males, Single Females. For all were
noted the age, place of birth, day of Baptism.

This set of registers is complete for Mission Santa Inés.
They tell a story all their own, and the information they contain between their flexible leather covers is indispensable for
relating the history of the Mission.

The title pages for the Registers of Baptism, Marriage,
and Deaths, were written by Fr. Presidente Estévan Tápis.
The text and form is alike in all three volumes save for the
words Baptism, Marriages, and Burials. The title page of the
Baptismal Register reads as follows:

"Blessed be Jesus!
First Book of Baptisms

"Of the New Mission of Our Lady Saint Agnes (Inés),
Virgin and Martyr, situated three leagues from the ocean,
intermediately between that of Purisima Concepcion and that
of Santa Barbara, on the site called by the natives Alajulapu.
It was founded at the expense and at the order of the Catholic
King of Spain and its Indies, the Señor Don Carlos IV (God
prosper him eternally), by the Rev. Fathers and Missionaries
Apostolic of the College of the propagation of the Faith of

SANTA INES AFTER MISSION PERIOD. NEOPHYTE VILLAGE AND RESERVOIR IN FORGROUND.

San Fernando de Mexico, to which the said Pious Monarch committed and delivered the conversion and administration of all these new Possessions. It was commenced on the day of the Wounds of the Seraphic Patriarch San Francisco, the 17th of September in the year 1804. On this day I, the undersigned Fr. Estévan Tápis, Presidente of these Missions of said College Apostolic, assisted by three other missionaries, blessed water, and with it the locality, dedicating it to God, our Lord, and then the great Cross, which we raised and venerated. We thereupon sang the Litany of All Saints. Then in an *enramada* (bower), which had been prepared and adorned with all the neatness possible, we sang the holy Mass, during which I preached to a number of *personas-de-razon*, among whom were present Don Raymundo Carrillo, lieutenant and commander of the royal presidio of Santa Barbara, and to a great multitude of neophytes who had come together for the function. Lastly we sang the *Te Deum Laudamus* with the accustomed orations. May it be to the greater honor and glory of God, the exaltation of His Most Holy Name, and for the welfare of souls.

"The first missionaries assigned by me on the authority of our holy College were the Rev. Fathers, Fr. José Antonio Calzada and Fr. José Romualdo Gutiérrez.

"This book consists of 297 folios for use and numbered, not counting the first and the last which remain blank. In testimony whereof I sign it.—Fr. Estévan Tápis."

The number and the baptismal name is always on the margin to the left. On the first page of the next leaf or folio begin the entries. The first entry reads as follows: "On the 17th of September, 1804, dedicated in honor of the Wounds of our holy Father San Francisco, in this Mission of Santa Inés, Virgin and Martyr, established on the same day, I baptized solemnly twenty-seven children, whom their pagan parents voluntarily offered for Baptism. First a male child six years of age, called in paganism Jaymel, native of the rancheria of Sotonucmu, and son of Mulusauta. I gave him the name Francisco de las Llagas. The sponsor for this and the eleven succeeding male children was Don Raymundo

Carrillo, lieutenant and commander of the royal presidio of
Santa Barbara, whom I reminded of the spiritual relation-
ship, and the other obligations which he contracted."

"Then follows as number 13, the first girl, Ynez, six years
of age, with 14 other little girls for whom the sponsor was
Doña Maria Ortega." All were entered singly, but Fr. Tápis
puts his signature only after the last of the 27 entries.

All these children, ranging from two months to six years
of age, received Baptism in the arbor or bower in which holy
Mass had been celebrated on the morning. The next entry,
number 28, notes that the Baptism on September 24, 1804,
was conferred *en la iglesia de esta Mision*, in the church of the
Mission, which had been meanwhile constructed. The subject
was Maria de Merced, three years old, and Fr. Gutiérrez
officiated.

Fr. Calzada two days later, September 26, had numbers
29-36. He also baptized the last candidates of the year, Nos.
97-112, on December 31.

The first white child, but recently born, was baptized on
December 27, 1805, and named Estéban Francisco. He was
the son of Joseph Bermudes, soldier of the presidio of Santa
Barbara, and Maria Estefana Villa, his wife. The Sponsors
were Francisco Ortega and Maria Antonia Ortega.

In June, 1806, Fr. Luis Gil y Taboada writes in the register, an expedition set out from the Mission of Santa Barbara
to survey the territory in the interior in search of sites suitable
for establishing Missions in accordance with orders from
Governor Don Joseph Joaquin de Arrillaga, who named for
chaplain the Rev. Fr. José Maria de Zalvidea. The latter in
the vicinity of Mission Santa Inés, Virgin and Martyr, baptized the following Indians *in articulo mortis*, Nos. 331-354."
Fr. Gil enters the names, ages, etc. The converts ranged
from 46 to 70 years of age. There were nineteen women and
five men. One woman at the rancheria of Sgene had seen
ninety-two winters.

Indians from the Islands opposite Santa Barbara frequently found their way to Mission Santa Inés, and joined

the community. The first to be baptized on November 10, 1814, was Isidoro, a boy 7 or 8 years of age. The mother was a pagan, and the father was not known. The child was a native of the rancheria of Elehuáchcuyu on the Island of Limú, (Santa Cruz), and had been sent by the mother to be baptized, the entry says. On the same day another boy, about five years old, from the rancheria of Cholochuch on the same island, was presented for Baptism. No others from there were baptized till April 8, 1815, when ten adult Indians, ranging from 20 to 30 years were baptized, all natives from the rancheria of Cheaumen on the same island. One of these was Aloya, captain or chief of that rancheria. After that Island Indians came frequently, as the register of Baptism notes.

In February, 1824, occured the unfortunate revolt of some of the neophytes. The first Baptism after the disturbance took place on March 25th, but at Mission Puris'ma. It was number 1228, and Fr. Blas Ordaz officiated. His first at Santa Inés is dated March 27, 1824, and is No. 1229. Then again, *en la Capilla de la Santa Iglesia de esta Mision de la Purisima*, Fr. Ordaz baptized No. 1230 on June 8th, and Fr. Rodriguez No. 1231 on June 14, 1824. No. 1232 on July 4, 1824, Fr. Ordaz entered at Santa Inés, and thereafter things took the usual course. The names of the various Fathers who were stationed at Mission Santa Inés or officiated there on any occasion will be found in the List at the end of chapter X.

The last of the Franciscans to officiate at Mission Santa Inés was the vice-rector of the College and Seminary, Fr. Francisco Sanchez, who entered his last Baptism on June 9, 1850. After that the Rev. Theodosio Boussier, C. SS. C., began making entries on July 1, 1850.

MARRIAGE REGISTER

The title page was written by Fr. Estévan Tápis. The text is similar to that of the baptismal register, save the change of Marriages for Baptisms. On the preceding fly-leaf, in keeping with his invariable custom, Fr. Comisario Prefecto

Vicente de Sarría has his *Auto-de-Visita,* or certificate of the canonical visitation of September 22, 1813, with Fr. Tápis countersigning as secretary. Likewise the *Auto-de-Visita* of July 1, 1816, is noted with Fr. Luis Gil y Taboada countersigning as secretary. These Autos-de Visita are found in all the Mission Registers on the first fly-leaf at all the Missions existing at his time.

The first marriage at Mission Santa Inés took place on December 16, 1804. The groom's name was Antonio de Padua Puyajaichet. The bride was Rafaela T. Esperanza. Both were neophytes of the Mission. All marriage regulations were strictly observed. Fr. Calzada officiated.

The first white couple to be married at the Mission were Joseph Vicente Ortega, son of Sergeant José Maria Ortega, with Maria Estefana, daughter of Sergeant Ignacio Olivera. The marriage took place on January 11, 1807, after the banns had been published also at Santa Barbara. Fr. Gil officiated.

On June 26, 1818, Fr. Sarría made his last visitation accompanied by Fr. Jayme Escudé as secretary.

The new Comisario Prefecto, Fr. Mariano Payeras, having Fr. José Sanchez as secretary, made the visitation and noted the same in the various books on July 27, 1821.

An interesting entry is No. 326. This notes that on November 5, 1822, José Juan Chapman, son of Daniel Chapman, native of Boston, was married to Maria Guadalupe Ortega, daughter of Vicente Ortega, native of the presidio (town) of Santa Barbara. Fr. Antonio Rodriguez officiated. This Mr. Chapman was a well and favorably known character of that period. He had been baptized at Mission San Buenaventura on June 24, 1822, by Fr. José Señan. Later he bought a house and planted a vineyard at Los Angeles, as Bancroft writes, "but still continued to do odd jobs at the Missions, being a jack-of-all trades, who apparently could make or repair anything that was needed. He was a great favorite with the friars, especially Fr. Sanchez, who declared it a marvel that one so long in the darkness of Baptist faith could give such example of true Catholic piety to older Christians. Among all the earliest pioneers of California there was no more attractive character, no more popular and useful man, than Joseph Chapman, the Yankee."[1]

Another marriage of some prominence was that of Nicholas August Den, single, of Waterford, Ireland, legitimate son of Manuel Den and Catherine O'Shea, who married Rafaela Rosa Antonia Hill, daughter of Daniel Hill and his wife Rafaela Ortega, on June 1, 1843. Fr. Juan Moreno officiated. It was entry No. 456.

The last entry of a Franciscan is No. 497 by Fr. J. J. Jimeno on March 12, 1850. Few marriages seem to have been contracted, owing to the meager Indian population that survived; for the next entry is dated September 24, 1851. The Rev. Eugene O'Connell, later first Bishop of Marysville, Cal., officiated.

BURIAL REGISTER

This volume of 298 folios is also complete, and the entries are continued to date. The title page is by Fr. Estévan Tápis. The first entry was made by Fr. Calzada on January 23, 1805, five months after the founding of the Mission. On that date he buried *en el cementerio de esta Mision* the body of an Indian girl infant named Cajetana.

On April 22, 1805, Fr. Gutiérrez made his first entry, when he noted the death of an Indian who had died and was buried at the rancheria. It was No. 9 in the list.

Of particular interest are the entries of the deaths of Fathers Calzada, Victoria, De la Cuesta, and Moreno, who were buried in the Church of the Mission of Santa Inés. The items are more complete than was customary with the Franciscans of those days. They will be found incorporated in the biographical sketches of the next chapter.

A forever sad event was the battle fought at the Mission. There is much confusion about the number of victims, which is rendered less intelligible by the Annual Report of December 31, 1824, the year of the revolt. Fr. Blaz writes under the

---

[1] Bancroft, *California*, vol. ii, p. 757.

caption of *Deaths* that during the year there died five male
Indian adults and fourteen children, eleven female adults and
four children, besides one white person, in all 35. Then seven
adults had been shot to death and had not received ecclesiastical burial; and one male adult and seven female adults had
died in camp and had been buried there without further
ecclesiastical ceremonies. This made 54 deaths to only 16
births in that year.

CEMETERY OF MISSION SANTA INES.

Yet the burial register notes only one dead in the revolt.
This was No. 950. Fr. Ordaz makes the entry thus: "On
March 21, 1824, in the cemetery of this Mission of Santa
Inés, I supplied the ceremonies for the ecclesiastical burial
of the body of *Sebastian, neophyte* of the Mission of Purisima
Concepcion, who had been buried lawfully in this cemetery
because he had been killed by violent hands, and the said
Mission lacked a missionary, as the troops had entered Mis-
sion Purisima and detained said missionary to serve them as
chaplain. In witness whereof, I sign. Fr. Blaz Ordaz.

Probably these deaths occurred in the region of San Emigdio whither the Indians from Santa Barbara fled after the attack on the Mission there by the soldiers. The deaths may have resulted from wounds received from the soldiers when the revolters attacked Mission Santa Inés. Where the victims of the fire came to their death is also not specified. It would seem that Carrillo would have reported such casualities to the commander of Santa Barbara, but no such report exists.

REGISTER OF CONFIRMATIONS

This begins with the usual initials *V. J. M. y J.*, which in English means *Blessed be Jesus, Mary, and Joseph*! Then follows this sentence: Confirmations bestowed by the Rev. Fr. Presidente and Vice-Prefecto, Fr. Narciso Durán, in the year 1834.

Fr. Durán was at that time the Presidente or Superior of the Franciscans from the College of San Fernando in the City of Mexico. He was also vice-prefect of the Commissary General in Mexico. As such Fr. Durán was authorized to administer the Sacrament of Confirmation in his district in California, from Mission Soledad to Mission San Diego, so long as there was no Bishop in California.

The text continues: "In the Confirmations celebrated by the Rev. Fr. Presidente in Lent of 1834, he conferred this Sacrament upon the following neophytes of this Mission of Santa Inés." Then follow the names of fifteen Indians. Fr. José Joaquin Jimeno certified to the fact by signing his name at the foot of the list, but he unfortunately forgot to add the exact date.

Bishop Garcia Diego for the first time visited Mission Santa Inés in September, 1842. On various dates from September 4th to September 15th, he confirmed 144 persons, mostly Indians of course. On his second visit, May 5, 1844, the Bishop confirmed 28 persons, and on August 4, 1844, he confirmed six more.

After the death of the Bishop, which occurred on April 30th, 1846, Fr. José Gonzales Rubio, his secretary, became Administrator of the Diocese. He also had the faculty to administer Confirmation. On various dates in June, 1849, therefore, Fr. Gonzales confirmed thirty-three persons, thus bringing up the number of Confirmations ever conferred at Mission Santa Inés to 226.

Rt. Rev. Joseph Sadoc Alemany, O. P., the second Bishop of California, for the first time confirmed eleven persons on August 22, 1851. The Bishop once more visited Santa Inés, and on December 30, 1852, confirmed four persons.

Rt. Rev. Thaddeus Amat, C. M., the first Bishop of Monterey and Los Angeles, frequently visited Mission Santa Inés. On the first occasion, March 2, 1856, he confirmed 17 persons, the names of whom were entered by the Rev. Juan Comapla, the pastor in charge.

Rt. Rev. Francis Mora for the first time notes his *Auto-de-Visita* on April 18, 1875, and again April 2, 1886.

CHAPTER IX.

The Mission Period for Santa Inés may be said to have
closed with the arrival of the Picpus Fathers and the with-
drawl of the Franciscans in May, 1850, as related in the sixth
chapter. The surrender was made by inventory signed by the
Rev. José Joaquin Jimeno, O. F. M., and the Rev. Theodosio
Boissier, C. SS. CC., on June 14, 1850. This document has
not as yet come to light.

It was fortunate that the seminary or college, independ-
ently of the Mission, possessed the lands granted by Governor
Micheltorena, and a good number of cattle the income from
which supplied the living for the professors and students.
Otherwise the inmates must have starved. Rt. Rev. Francisco Garcia Diego, O. F. M., the first Bishop of California,
indeed, after the confiscation of the Missions, in February,
1842, sought to provide a living for the clergy by directing
the faithful to contribute one-tenth of the produce of the lands
and one-tenth of the annual increase of the cattle for the
maintenance of the Bishop, the clergy, the seminary, and
divine worship; but the result was so discouraging that the
Bishop began to ail and finally died only four years later.

From a paper found in the Archives of Santa Barbara the
readers may infer what the situation was all over California
as regards the *Diézmo* or the contributions desired by the
Bishop. It is very likely that this information, which concerned Santa Inés in particular, was presented to the Picpus
Fathers when they took charge of the Mission in 1850, though
no date nor signature is attached. It may have been a part
of the missing inventory. Under the head *Apuntes sobre
Diézmos* the paper contains the following list of names and
the contributions or lack of contributions:

BEGINNING OF MISSION DECAY, AS EARLY AS 1865.

Antonio Maria Ortega paid nothing in various years.

Raymundo Carrillo, Gaspar Carrillo, Gaspar Oreña, José M. Covarrúbias, have paid nothing.

Octavian Gutiérrez owes two and one-half years contribution of cattle.

Ramon Malo owes the contribution of sheep from the year 1846 to 1849.

José Antonio Noriega owes for sheep since 1846.

Doña Magdalena for grape wine has not paid for various years.

José Manuel Ortega, José Dolores Ortega have paid nothing since 1846.

José Noriega has never paid for colts when he had them.

Joaquin Carrillo for 1849 and 1850 has paid nothing.

Anastasio Carrillo never paid anything for colts when he had them.

Juan Kays paid nothing for the years 1849 and 1850.

José Carrillo has paid nothing since he has "Santa Lucia."

José Maria Valenzuela paid for only one year.

Julian Foxen contributed from wheat, but from cattle nothing.

Miguel Valenzuela this and the previous year paid.

Gulliermo Hartnell for two years has paid nothing.

Miguel Cordero for young horses paid nothing.

Before the confiscation, while the Missions flourished, settlers were not called upon to contribute towards the maintenance of divine worship and its Ministers. They enjoyed the benefits of membership in the Church equally with the neophyte Indians, whose chapels and churches they attended and where they received the Sacraments in common with the neophytes. After Pio Pico and his gang had wiped out the Missions, rendered the Indians homeless and the missionaries penniless, the paisanos and others discovered that they themselves would be obliged to support the clergy and the churches if they and their families desired to share in the benefits of their Religion. Hence the introduction of the so-called *Diézmo* or contribution for the support of the Church and of the clergy. The ordinary Catholics of good will and good sense accepted the small burden as a matter of course. They realized that the Catholic Church is a Society the members of which must contribute towards the aims of the Society, just as members in any other society feel themselves bound to observe the regulations and obligations of their organization. Unfortunately, there were those, especially among the so-called upper classes, who had imbibed a great amount of irreligion and unscrupulous Liberalism the votaries of which at the present time are tyrannizing poor Mexico. This class of men disputed the right of the Church to collect anything for the support of her clergy and institutions. At Santa Inés the list reproduced on the preceding page proves that the former Mission was not blessed for having to count such characters among its flock. For details on the difficulties which the first Bishop of California encountered in this matter, the readers are referred to our *Missions and Missionaries*, volume iv, pages 239-240; 246 etc.; 608.

The Picpus Fathers remained at their post but one year. However, it is not possible to fix the dates of arrival and departure of priests at Santa Inés, because Baptisms were few, and their entries accordingly misleading. Father Migorel with Father Anaclet Lestrade of the same Congregation was sent to Los Angeles in order to open a school or college at the Plaza Church in Los Angeles. In 1853, owing to the great scarcity of priests, Father Migorel volunteered for the Missions of Lower California. He arrived there in 1854, and was assigned to a vast district the headquarters of which was Mulegé. There he labored heroically till April 17, 1859, when he passed to his reward.

The Rev. Eugene O'Connell, in the summer of 1851, succeeded Boissier and Migorel at Santa Inés, and had as assistant the Rev. Amable Petithomme. In November 1852, Archbishop José S. Alemany, O. P., recalled Father O'Connell, and gave him charge of St. Francis Church for the English-speaking people at San Francisco. In 1861 Father O'Connell was named Bishop of Grass Valley (now Sacramento), California.

The College near Santa Inés continued all along, but we could discover no particulars whatever until the arrival of the Christian Brothers.

The Rev. Juan Comapla, at the Mission, entered his first Baptism on April 25, 1854, as No. 1670. On that occasion he allows us a glimpse of information by signing the entry: *"Juan Comapla, Pbro.* (Presbitero) *y Vice Rector del Seminario Conciliar de California, Cura de las Misiones de Santa Inés y La Purisima."* He used the same titles until he made his last entry in the baptismal register, No. 1706, on March 7, 1857, when he signed *Juan Comapla, Pbro.* only. If he was Vice Rector, it is strange that he failed to name the Rector or the students anywhere.

The reason why so few Baptisms could be entered in the baptismal register is found in an undated note of the Archives of Mission Santa Barbara. It is reproduced here verbatim because of its historical value: "En Agosto de 1856 (hence during Father Comapla's term) habian en las jurisdicciones de *Santa Inés* y *La Purisima* Indios existentes:—el numero total 164 repartidos como sigue:

En la *Zanja Cota* (Reservation now)	Adultos casados	21
	Adultas viudas	11
	Adultos solteros	4
Muchachos............	hasta 14 años	19
	Total	55
	Adultas casadas	23
	Adultas viudas	9
	Adultas solteras	3
Muchachas............	hasta 12 años	19
	Total	54

MOST REV. BISHOP THADDEUS AMAT, C. M., D. D.

Nota. Las dos casadas en exceso son porque sus maridos estan ausentes.
En esta fecha habian viejos de 50 años para arriba–8 adultos y 1 adulta.

"	"	" 60	"	"	" –5	"	" 2 adultas.
"	"	" 70	"	"	" –2	"	" 2 "
"	"	" 80	"	"	" –3	"	" 5 "

This means that of the Santa Inés Indians 109 survived
and lived near the ancient Mission. Of the neophytes belonging to Mission Purisima only fifty-five still lived, were scattered in the Purisima district, and were attended in their
spiritual needs by the priests at Santa Inés.

At the same period the *Alcaldes* were:
Rafael, de buena conducta;
Luis, de excelente conducta;
Tomas, de costumbres regulares;
Pablo, de costumbres regulares.

The *Vaqueros* were:
Benevento, que cuida dos caballos y yeguas, es muy honrado
y trabajado;
Odorico, es muy bueno;
Basilio, es muy bueno;
Angel, es muy bueno;
Juan Bautista, es muy bueno.

A close examination of *The Catholic Directory* reveals the
fact that the Seminary at Santa Inés figured in the reports for
thirty years. The first report communicated by the Rt. Rev.
José Sadoc Alemany, O. P., Bishop of Monterey, California,
reads as follows: "The Seminary of the diocese is at Santa
Inés, about 400 miles from San Francisco." Nothing more.

For the year 1852 the report reads: "Diocesan College
and Seminary at Santa Inés. Rev. Eugene O'Connell and
Rev. Amable Petithomme." No students mentioned.

In 1853 the Rev. T. Piret, C. SS. CC., was in charge, but
no students nor teachers are named.

Meanwhile the diocese, which comprised the whole State
of California, was divided. San Francisco became an Archdiocese; the central and southern part of the State was made
a diocese with headquarters at Monterey as before. The
Bishop of Monterey was the Rt. Rev. Thaddeus Amat, C. M.,

who in 1854 reported to the Directory as follows: Diocesan Seminary and College of Our Lady of Guadalupe at Santa Inés has about 12 students and two Professors. Rev. John Comapla, Superior." The institution accordingly received the title of Our Lady of Guadalupe and was so named ever after.

In 1855 only ten students attended the College, with Rev. Ciprian Rubio as Superior. Thereafter more boys came to the school. In 1858 as many as 21 students were enrolled; and in 1859 there were 25 with Father Rubio still Superior.

In 1862 Father Rubio was transferred to Mission San Juan Bautista. Thereafter no priest was noted in the Directory as connected with the College. For the years 1863 to 1865 only 16 students boarded at the institution. Who the teachers or managers were was not stated.

At last in 1868, the Directory informs us, the Institution was conducted by Franciscan Brothers. This statement is found in successive years till 1874, when the number of students is reported as fifty, and Brother Paschal noted as Director. These Brothers continued three years longer. Then, in 1877, Archbishop Alemany asked the Provincial of the Christian Brothers, Brother Justin, to take charge of the place and carry on the boarding and day school. The Provincial agreed and sent Brothers Baptist and Julian. The former stayed for one year. Brother Walter was then sent up for his health, and to act as Superior and manager. He recovered his health and remained to the last.

"The College was one and one-half miles from Mission Santa Inés," Brother Walter on inquiry informs us: "When the Christian Brothers were appointed the institution was in charge of the Franciscan Brothers Paschal Doran and Bernard from Brooklyn, N. Y. Rev. John B. McNally, later of Oakland, was pastor of the district and chaplain of the College. The Franciscan Brother Paschal Doran died as sexton of Father McNally at Oakland."

Thirty-six thousand acres of land belonged to the College, and was known as the College Ranch. Governor Manuel

Micheltorena, on petition of the first Bishop, Rt. Rev. Francisco Garcia Diego y Moreno, O. F. M., granted the land for educational purposes in the name of the Mexican Government.

Accordingly, when Archbishop Alemany desired to sell the land and close the school, it required an Act of Congress to permit the sale. This was effected in 1881, the Archbishop for his diocese sold 20,000 acres, the share coming to him, and turned over the other 16,000 acres to the Bishop of Monterey. Thereupon, 1882, the Christian Brothers retired.

The average number of boarding boys, Brother Walter relates, was about 25 to 36 nearly all from San Francisco. There were but very few day pupils. The Rev. Fr. Francisco Sanchez, O. F. M., used to come up at least once a year for the sake of the Mexicans and Spaniards."

The reference to Father McNally solves a puzzle which lingered with us for nearly twenty years. In passing through the territory formerly covered with Indian rancherias, we found at Sisquoc and Lompoc neat little churches built after the same style. Each had two little towers, and the tiny vestry was in the rear of the altar. These chapels also contained an organ loft. We were told that these little churches had been erected by Father McNally of Oakland, California, for the English-speaking settlers. His name was not mentioned in any of the Mission registers of either Purisima Concepcion or Mission Santa Inés. Father McNally, under the jurisdiction of the Archbishop of San Francisco, had his headquarters at the College Ranch. From there he attended the settlers all around even as far as Guadalupe, and induced them to erect the churches to suit the number of families. He must have had occasion to baptize or perform other priestly functions and then entered them in his personal registers or at his parish church in Oakland. We met the Rev. Father but once on occasion of the unveiling of the marble slabs placed over the graves of deceased Franciscan Fathers in the sanctuary of the Mission Church at San Miguel. At that time we knew nothing of his connection with the College of Guadalupe, and

REMAINDER OF GUADALUPE COLLEGE IN 1904.

so missed obtaining full and exact information at first hand. "After the Christian Brothers left," Brother Walter concluded his notes on the College of Guadalupe. "Mr. Mullaney was put in charge to act as subagent for the sale of the property." When we saw it about thirty years later, the college building was in ruins.

Miss Catherine Donohue, daughter of an old settler informs us: "My father, Thomas James Donohue, left Gilroy, California, in November, 1882, for Santa Inés to buy land from the College grant, but the land had already been taken off the market when he arrived. Father Michael Lynch had written us to come, and he also asked us to live at the Old Mission."

Father Lynch had succeeded Father Basso at the Mission, but lived at the College, and from there attended the English-speaking settlements by turns, as we shall learn presently.

CHAPTER X.

Fr. Joseph Calzada is mentioned for the first time in a letter of Governor Fages to Fr. Presidente Fermín de Lasuén on October 12, 1787, as having arrived at Monterey. He must have landed on October 10th or 11th. He officiated at a Baptism for the first time on February 21, 1788, at Mission San Gabriel, and continued there till October 19, 1792, except that from September 20, 1788, to January 12, 1789, he was at Mission Santa Barbara, probably on account of ill health. From San Gabriel Fr. Calzada was transferred to Mission Purisima. On his way he stopped at Mission Santa Barbara, and there on November 3, 1792, officiated at a Baptism. At Purisima he entered his first Baptism on November 22, 1792, and remained there till appointed to found Mission Santa Inés. It seems that he was ever struggling against ill health; for from the end of July, 1796, to May, 1798, he was absent in Mexico to recuperate. He would occasionally visit Santa Barbara Mission, as his signature appears there in June, August and September, 1798, and July, 1803. His last entry in the register of Purisima is dated August 25, 1804.

After the founding of Mission Santa Inés on September 17, 1804, he visited Santa Barbara Mission but once, March to April, 1806. He was also present at the dedication of the new church of Mission San Buenaventura on September 9, 1809. His last entry in the baptismal register of Mission Santa Inés was written on September 14, 1810. Thereafter Fr. Calzada is enumerated in the official *Lista* of 1813 and 1814 as supernumerary. Fr. Presidente José Señan on October 1, 1813, in the *Lista* writes: "There are two supernumeraries, Fr. José Antonio Calzada and Fr. Vicente Oliva. The former is at Mission Santa Inés, so completely paralyzed, that he is unable to move." Similarly, Fr. Señan reports on April 17,

1814. Death at last relieved poor Fr. Calzada of his sufferings on December 23, 1814. The entry of his burial in the *Libro de Difunctos*, or Burial Register, is very complete, wherefore it is transcribed here in full.

"No. 414, Fr. José Antonio Calzada. On the 24th day of December, 1814, in the church which serves as such temporarily, with the assistance of the Rev. Fathers Francisco Xavier Uria, missionary in charge of the Mission of Santa Inés, Fr. Antonio Ripoll of Mission Purisima, and Fr. Ramon Olbés of Mission Santa Barbara, I gave ecclesiastical burial to the body of the Rev. Fr. José Antonio Calzada, Missionary Apostolic of the College of San Fernando de Mexico, member of the (Franciscan) Province of Santa Helena de la Florida. He made his profession (vows) at the convent of Purisima Concepcion in the City of Havana on the third of February, 1780. He was born in the City of Trinidad,[1] in the parish

church of which he was also baptized on the 24th of November, 1760, which baptismal entry is to be found in Libro Sexto de Bautismos de los Españoles of the said parish on page 195. He was the son of the married couple Don José Calzada and Doña Micaela de Cala. From the Province of Santa Helena he went to Mexico, and was incorporated in the aforesaid College of San Fernando de Mexico in which city he was also ordained priest on the 18th of December, 1784. In 1787 he was assigned to the Missions of Alta California. In the year

---

[1] Trinidad, a city on the south side of the Island of Cuba, situated on a small river of the same name, 178 miles south-east from Havana. Cuba and the Franciscan missionaries in Florida, with headquarters at St. Augustine Florida, constituted the Franciscan Province of Santa Helena which existed before the Pilgrim Fathers reached the shore of Massachussetts in 1620.

1804 he founded this Mission of Santa Inés, laboring with indefatigable zeal for its spiritual and material progress until the year 1812, when he became entirely incapacitated in consequence of a stroke of apoplexy which rendered him unable to serve as missionary. He died after having received the Sacraments of Penance, Holy Viaticum, and Extreme Unction. In witness whereof I signed in the Mission of Santa Inés on December 24, 1814. Fr. Estévan Tápis."

Fr. Marcos Antonio Saizar de Vitoria y Odriozola, who however always signed himself simply Fr. Marcos Antonio de Vitoria, also died at Santa Inés. The burial entry for this noble friar is so detailed and complete that we hardly need add anything more. It reads thus: "No. 1298. Fr. Marcos Antonio de Vitoria.—On July 26, 1836, in the church of this Mission of Santa Inés, with the assistance of the Rev. Missionary Fathers Felipe Arroyo de la Cuesta and Fr. José Joaquin Jimeno, the former of Mission Purisima Concepcion, and the other of this Mission, the Rev. Fr. Ramon Abella, missionary of the Mission of San Luis Obispo, gave ecclesiastical burial to the body of the Rev. Fr. Marcos Antonio Saizar de Vitoria y Odriozola, missionary of this Mission, who was a member of the holy Province of Cantabria. He was born in the City of Vitoria, capital of the Province of Alava, Spain, in 1760, as the legitimate son of Miguel Saizar de Vitoria, and his wife Maria Andrea Odriozola, inhabitants of said city. He received the holy habit on September 11, 1776, and made his vows in the *convento grande capitular* of our Father San Francisco in the same city of Vitoria. In 1780 he received the Minor Orders at Calahorra (Province of Logrono), and in 1781 he was ordained subdeacon at Saragoza. In 1782 he was ordained deacon at Jaca, Aragon; and finally in 1784 he was elevated to the priesthood at Saragoza. After he had been stationed in turn at Bilbao, Aranzazú, Piedroba, and lastly at the Recollect convent of Purisima Concepcion, where he was master of novices, Fr. Marcos Antonio passed over to North America to the College of San Fernando de Mexico in 1804. In 1805 he came to these Missions of Alta California landing at San

Francisco. Obedience destined him first for the Mission of Santa Barbara, then for that of San Buenaventura, thereupon for that of San Fernando Rey, thence for that of Purisima, and lastly for this Mission of Santa Inés. In all these places he exercised the apostolic ministry with great zeal for souls, and with exemplary edification of the neophytes, soldiers, people of the country, and foreigners who knew him. He merited for himself the respect, attention, appreciation, and eulogies of everybody, even of the enemies of Catholicism, on account of his virtues, charity, supreme, continual mortification, and religious affability. He is indeed worthy of everlasting memory.

"He died at 1:45 in the morning of July 25, 1836, having received with all humility, tenderness, devotion, fervor, and great conformity to the will of God the holy Sacrament of Penance many times, and likewise that of the Holy Eucharist, once as Viaticum, and of Extreme Unction. Likewise there were applied the two Indulgences of Benedict XIV and of the Order, all in the holy Church down to the Recommendation of the Soul. He thus secured from the Lord by his great merits the singular grace of commending his spirit into Divine Hands in the very week in which he was performing the prescribed acts for gaining the Universal Jubilee granted by His Holiness Gregory XVI on the Pope's accession to the Pontifical throne in order to implore the divine assistance in these last calamitous times. Fr. Marcos Antonio is interred in the church below the sanctuary on the Epistle side, close to the Communion railing. In witness whereof we, the above mentioned missionaries assisting have signed this.—Fr. Felipe Arroyo de la Cuesta.—Fr. José Joaquin Jimeno."

This magnificent tribute in the hand of Fr. J. J. Jimeno was well deserved, as the reader will find verified by consulting the pages of the respective local histories whose Missions were fortunate enough to profit by the ministrations of Fr. Vitoria. The Fathers, generally, spell his name Victoria, but Fr. Marcos Antonio always wrote it Vitoria, as the facsimile signature proves.

At the Chapter held in the College of San Fernando, Mexico, December 3, 1836, the Community not having received the notice of his death, though it had occurred five months previously, good Father Vitoria was given five votes for the office of Discreto or Councillor of the College, and declared elected.

Fr. Jimeno on the day of Fr. Vitoria's death hastened a messenger down to Santa Barbara with a circular giving the details of his beautiful end. Fr. Narciso Durán, then Superior of the Missions of Southern California, passed the circular on to the next Mission, but under the same date of July 25, 1836, added the following tribute: "My beloved Fathers. Already it has pleased the Lord to take from us the principal column of the Seraphic edifice of this California. He has taken away from us the Angel in the flesh, or the man without flesh, the venerable and saintly Fr. Marcos Antonio de Victoria, of whose holy, religious, and angelical life we are all witnesses. Indeed, My Fathers, we are all witnesses of that most profound humility, of that angelical purity, and of the seraphic piety which have so much adorned the venerable deceased, and who with these and all other virtues befitting to a Religious of St. Francis has adorned so much this California so that his memory in this country will be eternal. It is very likely that he needs not our suffrages; nevertheless let us apply them to him in order to comply with our religious agreement. The Rev. Fathers of San Diego will see that this (notice) passes on to the Rev. Fathers and Brothers of Lower California (Dominicans) until it reaches the hands of their Rev. Fr. Presidente, and they will supplicate this prelate to return it at his convenience to the prelate here.—Fr. Narciso Durán."

The agreement to which Fr. Narciso makes reference bound every Franciscan and Dominican in California to celebrate twenty holy Masses for the soul of any friar who might die in the Missions. (See *The Missions and Missionaries*, vol. i, p. 305; vol. ii, pp. 67, 170; vol. iv, p. 708.)

The circular was signed in turn at Santa Barbara by Fr. Antonio Jimeno, Fr. Buenaventura Fortuni, and the Very

Rev. J. A. Alejo Bachelot of Los Angeles on the same July 25; by Fr. Blas Ordaz of San Buenaventura, on the same July 25; at San Fernando by Fr. Pedro Cabot, on July 26; by Fr. Thomas Esténaga on July 27 at San Gabriel; and by Fr. José Maria de Zalvidea at San Juan Capistrano on July 31, 1836.

In his *Biographical Sketches* of the Friars, Fr. Comisario Prefecto Vicente de Sarría, on November 5, 1817, writes of Fr. Vitoria: "Fr. Marcos Antonio de Vitoria, the capital of Province of Alava. In the convent of our Father San Francisco in the same city, belonging to the holy Province of Cantabria, he received the habit on September 11, 1776. In said Province of his, he was Visitador of the Third Order for four years and a half, and master of novices for ten and a half years. He embarked on June 20, 1803, for the College of San Fernando de Mexico, and reached there on September 9th of the same year. In March 1805 the *Discretorio* and the Fr. Guardian sent him to these Missions. At that of Santa Barbara, one of them, and at its adjacent presidio he served somewhat more than a year. Soon after he was assigned to that of San Buenaventura, where until this day he was stationed as missionary. Owing to his innocence and purity which seem to constitute his true character, and for the general edification, which results from them his merit must not be placed among those of inferior class, although he may not do as much as many others. Believing that he could not fulfil all the duties of a missionary, and seeing himself afflicted with various serious bodily maladies, so much so that at one time they threatened to end his life, he solicited to be retired for some time, and only that I assured him that there was no priest available to take his place, that he should do what he could in accordance with his weak constitution, I succeeded in quieting him and leaving him resigned."

The successor of Fr. Sarría, Fr. Mariano Payéras, in his *Sketches* dated December 31, 1820, says that Fr. Marcos Victoria was then 60 years of age. Then after mentioning dates already noted, he writes: "His most eminent merit is his distinguished virtue, and his blessed simplicity."

His name appears in the Registers of Mission Santa Barbara from October 5, 1805, to June 30, 1807; then on visits September to December, 1807; March, 1808; and August 28, 1824; at Mission San Buenaventura July 12, 1806 to June 20, 1824; at Mission San Fernando, August 6, 1806, January 11, 1816; January 25, 31, 1817; December 12, 1817; April 11, 1820; at Purisima, from December 18, 1824, to June 19, 1835. Fr. Vitoria was also present at the dedication of the church of Mission San Juan Capistrano, and sang the High Mass on September 8, 1806.

Fr. Felipe Arroyo de la Cuesta. Of this much afflicted Father Fr. Comisario Prefecto Sarría wrote in his *Sketches* on November 5, 1817; "Fr. Felipe Arroyo de la Cuesta is 37 years and six months old. He is a native of the Villa de Cubo in Old Castile and Archdiocese of Burgos. He received the holy habit in the convent of the said city and in the Franciscan Province of the same name of Burgos on August 3, 1796. On September 2, 1804, he embarked at Cádiz for the College of San Fernando de Mexico, whence he set out on December 14, 1807, for these Missions of Alta California. From the beginning he was located as missionary at Mission San Juan Bautista, where he has continued to this day. He applied himself most assiduously to the learning of the respective languages with such success that I doubt that there is another who has reached the same proficiency in understanding and describing its intricate syntax. He even reduced to some sort of rules the confusing formations of its verbs, adverbs and the rest of the parts of speech which I understand may serve likewise for other Missions; for, notwithstanding that their languages are very different, and many of them two and three idioms without leaving the own district, they preserve their analogy without regard to expressing their ideas. I have animated him to compose a work on the subject. He has labored, as I understand, with good success, wherefore he may succeed in the work. In the midst of all this he has been afflicted for four or five years with grave rheumatic pains, which for a long time prevented him from celebrating holy Mass; but in the rest of the duties

he served in the regular management of the needs of the
Mission, especially attending to the instructions which his
said knowledge of the language made it easier for him so far
as his health aids him."

Fr. Sarría's successor, Fr. Mariano Payéras, three years
later, December 31, 1820, wrote of Fr. Arroyo: "He is 40
years of age, and his merit is above the average in his aptitude
and disposition. Although in itself it is very high, it promises
nothing owing to his grave infirmities which are already habitual and which for years have made him think at least of
death.

On the arrival of the Franciscans from Zacatecas College,
who accepted the Missions north of Soledad, Fr. Arroyo was
transferred to Mission Santa Inés, staying on the way a little
while at each of the Missions of San Miguel, San Luis Obispo,
and one year at Mission Purisima, arriving at Santa Inés in
1836 more crippled than ever. Yet he was a methodical man,
and therefore brought desired order in the various books of
the Mission outside the registers, thus serving history materi-
ally. He finally passed to his reward in 1840. The Burial
Register says of him: "No. 1400. On September 20, 1840,
died at this Mission the Rev. Fr. Felipe Arroyo de la Cuesta,
missionary of this Mission of Santa Inés. He was born at the
Villa de Cubo in Spain, in the province of Burgos, district of
Bureba, a section of Santa Maria de Rivarredonde. He was
baptized in the parish church del S. S. Millan on May 2nd,
1780, three days after his birth. His parents were Don Matias
Arroyo and Doña Isabel de la Cuesta, his wife. At the age of
16 years, on August 3, 1796, he received the habit of our
Father San Francisco in the *convento grande* of the holy Province of Burgos, and on August 6, the following year he made
his vows. In the year 1804, already ordained priest, he passed
over to North America for the College of San Fernando de
Mexico, where he remained four years exercising his apostolic
ministry with exactitude. In 1808 he pleaded with ardor for
permission to come to these Missions of Alta California, and
with the permit of the prelate he came and was assigned for

the Mission of San Fernando. This arrangement did not take effect, because owing to circumstances that occurred it was more expedient to destine him as missionary for Mission San Juan Bautista. Here he stayed till 1833, when on account of the arrival of the Zacatecan Fathers, he went down to that of San Miguel, and a little while after to that of San Luis Obispo. In 1835 he went to Purisima, and in 1836 to this Mission of Santa Inés. In these latter Missions he labored little because of his painful infirmity which prevented him from walking, and even from resting for a length of time. On this account he did not celebrate holy Mass; but at the Mission of San Juan Bautista, where he was stationed about 25 years, he toiled with great zeal. There he enjoyed the holy satisfaction of seeing converted through his ardor and energy exceedingly great numbers of Gentiles, whom like those converted previously he catechized and instructed perfectly, as well through his persistence as through the knowledge he had of the various languages of the Indians..—

"His last illness was long and painful. During the same he received repeatedly the holy Sacraments of Penance, Holy Eucharist, and once that of Extreme Unction. He died very much conformed to the will of God. His body was interred in the church of this Mission on the Gospel side of the sanctuary on September 22, 1840. In witness whereof I signed, Fr. José Joaquin Jimeno."

Fr. José Ramon Abella. Of this good Father the Rev. Fr. Comisario Prefecto Sarría writes on November 5, 1817: "Fr. Ramon Abella is 53 years and 4 months old. His native town is the Pueblo de Monforte in the Archdiocese of Zaragoaz in the kingdom of Aragon. He received the holy habit in the convent of Nuestra Señora de Jesus of said city of Zaragoza on March 6, 1784. On September 9, 1794, he set out from the convent of San Antonio de Mora, where he was the vicar of the house at the time, in order to embark at Cádiz for the College of San Fernando de Mexico, which he did in the beginning of 1795. Since 1798, when he set out for these lively Missions of the College, he served with much fidelity in the administration of that of our Father San Francisco and the presidio of the same name to this present epoch. He is according to my estimation, as well as for his character a sincere religious. As experience shows with his Indians, the number of those he has baptized, and of those that died in that Mission, and judging from his solicitude and patience required and the attention also to the presidio, his merit is that of the best laborers in these Missions."

Fr. Ramon Abella

Fr. Sarría's successor, Fr. Mariano Payéras, on December 31, 1820, wrote of Fr. Abella: "He is fifty-six years of age. His merit is great, and his aptitude for the complete discharge of the ministry among the whites and Indians, and for one or the other office in the Order."

The entry for the deceased Fr. Abella reads as follows: "No. 1437. Fr. Ramon Abella, missionary of Purisima Concepcion. In the year of the Lord, 1842, on the 24th day of the month of May, there died at this Mission of Santa Inés the Rev. Fr. Ramon Abella, missionary of the Mission of Purisima. He was born on May 28, 1764, in the Pueblo called Montforte in the Province of Aragon. He received the holy habit of our Father San Francisco on March 6, 1784, and made his vows on March 7, 1785, in the convent of Nuestra Señora de Jesus at Saragoza. He received the Minor Orders on March 2, 1787; subdeaconship on December 22, 1787; deaconship on May 17, 1788; and the priesthood on September 20, 1788. In 1795, being preacher and confessor, he crossed over to this North America, and was assigned to the College of San Fernando de Mexico, where he stayed and discharged the apostolic ministry laudably for about three years. In 1798 he turned to these Missions of Alta California, where he was stationed and for 44 years administered various Missions, two of which with a presidio. In these establishments he devoted himself religiously to perform with such exactitude the spiritual ministry that he edified and was even admired for his indefatigable zeal. Already worn out and enfeebled, and deeply saddened on account of the deplorable state of the last two Missions in which he had been stationed, he retired to this Mission of Santa Inés in order to end the few days that remained of his life in the midst of his brethern so that he might receive the spiritual helps. These he received, confessing many times, and receiving the Sacred Eucharist, and the Sacrament of Extreme Unction, and finally dying with great tranquillity, on the day, month, and year stated. His body was interred next to the sanctuary on the Epistle side about two varas distant from the wall. In witness whereof I sign this. Fr. José Joaquin Jimeno."

Fr. Abella's name appears for the first time in the baptismal register of San Francisco Mission on July 15, 1798, and for the last time on April 10, 1819. During that period he baptized once at Santa Clara on September 19, 1801; then at San José August 28, 1811; June 1, 1815; May 9, 1816; August 1, 1817. He was transferred to Mission San Carlos and there for the first time baptized on July 30, 1819; the last time on April 21, 1833, meanwhile once also at Mission San Luis Obispo on November 20, 1820. On his way to San Luis Obispo he baptized on June 8, 1833 at San Antonio. At San Luis Obispo he began his entries in the register on July 24, 1834; his last was November 24, 1841. During this period he baptized at Purisima July 25, 1836; December 9, 1839. Fr. Abella was stationed at Mission Purisima and baptized for the first time in January, 1842.

Fr. Juan Moreno was the last Franciscan to die at Mission Santa Inés. The burial entry gives the details about his antecedents so far as known. It reads thus: "No. 1528. On December 28, 1845, the Rev. Fr. Vice-Rector, Fr. Francisco Sanchez, with the assistance of the Fr. Rector and all the alumni of the College, gave ecclesiastical burial to the body of the Rev. Fr. Juan Moreno, missionary of this Mission of

Santa Inés, and professor in the Tridentine Seminary. He
was born on January 27, 1799, at Montenegro, town of Xioja
in Old Castile. He received the habit of our Father San
Francisco in the Franciscan Province of the Holy Gospel,
Mexico. He received the Minor Orders from the Most Rev.
Archbishop, Don Pedro de Fonte, on June 15, 1821; subdeaconship from the same Archbishop in the city of Toluca,
on September 21, 1822; deaconship on 24".................
There in the register about half a page remains blank, probably with the intention of filling out the space with remaining
dates.

    From the Biennial Report of March 1828, however, we
know that Fr. Juan Moreno came to California in January
1828, and seems to have landed at Santa Barbara early in that
month in the company of Fr. Antonio Jimeno, with whom he
bears the distinction of being the last recruit for California
from the College of San Fernando. While Fr. Jimeno was sent
to Santa Cruz, Fr. Juan Moreno was stationed at Santa
Barbara, and made his first entry in the Mission register on
January 26, 1828. His last is dated February 2, 1829. Then
it appears he changed places with Fr. Antonio Jimeno, who
for the first time enters on January 28, 1829, whereas Fr.
Moreno made his first entry at Santa Cruz on October 3, 1829,
although he arrived there on August 8, 1829. His last entry
at Santa Cruz is dated October 30, 1830. He was then appointed for Mission San Juan Bautista to aid the crippled
Fr. Arroyo, and made his first entry there on February 22,
1830. He was already in ill health himself, for Fr. Arroyo on
December 31, 1830, reported: "Fr. Juan Moreno is not in
good health; but he is cured of his scrofulas by means of
sajadas." He stayed at San Juan Bautista with Fr. Arroyo

until the arrival of the Zacatecan Fathers. Fr. Arroyo left
there May 14, 1833.

Rev. Alexander Buckler, as the restorer of the Misssion
buildings, deserved exceedingly well of Mission Santa Inés.
It is therefore meet that his memory be perpetuated with
those of the Franciscan missionaries who died and were
buried here, particularly because he had been a member of
the Third Order of St. Francis.

Father Buckler was born on the Lower Rhine, Germany,
on May 23, 1855. He arrived in America as a student on
June 3, 1877, and was ordained priest at St. Meinrad's Bene-
dictine Abbey, Indiana, on May 19, 1883. After serving as
parish priest in Minnesota, he came to California on September 9, 1903, and was given charge of Our Lady of Sorrows
Church, Santa Barbara, to enable the Rev. Polidor Stockman,
the Rector, to visit Europe. In July, 1904, Father Buckler
was appointed pastor of Mission Santa Inés and depending
stations. In this capacity he served till November 2, 1924,
when ill health compelled him to resign his charge. Eventually
he died on March 7, 1930. The remains were interred in
Calvary Cemetery, Santa Barbara. R. I. P.

Resident and Visiting Franciscans and Their
Successors at Mission Santa Inés

Fr. Estévan Tápis, Founder, September 17, 1804.
Fr. José Antonio Calzada, September 17, 1804, to No. 529,
   September 14, 1810.
Fr. Romualdo Gutiérrez, September 17, 1804, to No. 311,
   July 19, 1806.
   Fr. Luis Antonio Martinez, October 24, 1804.
   Fr. Marcos Amestoy, January 19, 1805; March 22, 1810.
   Fr. Juan Cortés, May 9, 1805.
   Fr. Tápis, June 18, 1805; August 2, 1806; June 29, Septem-
   ber 12, 1808.
Fr. Luis Gil de Taboada, August 1, 1806, to No. 489, Feb-
   ruary 13, 1810.

Fr. F. X. Uria, No. 442, December 12, 1808, to No. 1227, January 29, 1824.

Fr. Felipe Arroyo de la Cuesta, December 26, 1810.

Fi. Ramon Olbés, No. 623, November 20, 1812, to Feburary and March, 1813.

Fr. Tápis, No. 662, October 13, to No. 698, December 12, 1814.

Fr. Antonio Ripoll, January 22, 1815; July 30, 1822.

Fr. Roman Ulibarri, No. 702, Feburary 23, 1815, to No. 787, November 20, 1819.

Fr. Ramon Olbés, March 13, 1816.

Fr. Gil de Taboada, July 2, 1816; March 16, 1817.

Fr. Vicente P. Oliva, April 19, to May 17, 1819.

Fr. Ant. Rodríguez, June 5, 1819; October 25, 1820; April, November, 1821.

Fr. José Sanchez, June 20, 1820; November, December, 1821.

Fr. Francisco Gonzalez Ibárra, October 17, 1820; June 20, 1822.

Fr. Antonio Rodríguez, January, 1822; December 2, 1822.

Fr. Blas Ordáz, June 2, 9, 1823.

Fr. Blas Ordáz, No. 1228, March 25, 1824, to April 3, 1833, No. 1336.

Fr. José Moreno, Feburary 11, 1829; January 9, 14, 1834.

Fr. José Joaquín Jiméno, No. 1337, May 14, 1833, to May 31, 1842, No. 1425.

Fr. Felipe Arroyo de la Cuesta, December 1836; June, July, 1837.

Fr. Juan Moreno, No. 1480, April 10, 1842, No. 1480, to April 2, 1844, No. 1528.

Rev. José Miguel Gómez, August 26, 1842, No. 1499, Indian child named Zeferino.

Fr. J. J. Jimeno, No. 1513, May 17, 1843, to December 8, 1849.

Rev. J. M. Gomez, January, September, 1843.

Fr. Francisco Sanchez, December 10, 1848, No. 1607, to June 9, 1850, No. 1631.

Father Sanchez was the last Franciscan at Santa Inés.

Rev. Theodosio Boussier, C .SS. CC., July 1, 1850, to October
    7, 1850.

Rev. Felipe Migorel, C. SS. CC., January 4, to January 15,
    1851.

Rev. Eugene O'Connell, No. 1640 November 8, 1851, to No.
    1653, October 31, 1852.

Rev Amable Petithomme, C. SS. CC., November 5, 1851.

Rev. Lempfried, O. M. I., January 20, 1853, to August 7, 1853.

Rev. C. Victor Piret, September 18, 1853, to March 26, 1854.

Rev. Juan Comapla, April 25, 1854, to March 7, 1857.

Rev. Cipriano Rúbio, April 15, 1856, to January 16, 1862.

Rev. Miguel Bacca, February 2, to December 20, 1862.

Rev. Juan Basso, January 7, 1863, to August 24, 1865.

Rev. Joaquin Bot, April 2, 1865, to August 24, 1867.

Rev. Juan Basso, September 13, 1867, to April 9, 1875.

    Rev. James Croke, September 28, 1873.

Rev. Michael Lynch, June 15, 1875, to December 23, 1886.

Rev. Patrick Farrelly, March 11, 1888, to November 8, 1890.

Rev. F. M. Lack, April 12, 1891, to September 4, 1903.

Rev. Thomas King, September 29, 1903, to July 21, 1904.

Rev. Alexander Buckler, July 21, 1904, to November 2, 1924.

    Rev. P. A. Quinn, October, 10, 1922, to April 21, 1923.

    Rev. Gab. Ryan, October 21, to November 18, 1923.

    Rev. L. Bourke, August 2, to November 20, 1924.

The Rev. A. Buckler resigned his charge on account of ill
health. Thereupon Most Rev. John J. Cantwell, D. D., the
Bishop of the Diocese of Los Angeles and San Diego, turned
over Mission Santa Inés to the Capuchin Fathers, who took
possession on November 20, 1924.

Fr. Albert Biddy, O. M. Cap., from November 20, 1924, to
    Feburary 19, 1925, when he died at St. Francis Hospital,
    Santa Barbara.

Fr. Stephen Murtagh, O. M. Cap., November 20, 1924, to
    end of 1925.

Fr. Casimir Buttler, O. M. Cap., 1925 to

CHAPTER XI.

Resuming the narrative concerning Mission Santa Inés,
we find that the priests succeeded one another without note-
worthy incident down to the administration of the Rev. Juan
Basso, 1867-1875. While the white settlers gradually increased in numbers, however, the neophyte Indian population
was steadily approaching extinction. The white man's
whiskey, and the easy communication with the pagan Tulare
Indians were playing havoc with the surviving remnants of
Mission Santa Inés and of Mission Purisima who were drawn
closer together near Mission Santa Inés.

One of the Tulareños named Cayetano proved especially
vicious and arrogant. He would behave insolently to Father
Basso himself. One day, at the mouth of Alisal Cañon,
Cayetano attacked a Mission Indian named Jose, and killed
him. José Cardona, another Mission Indian, tried to shield
Jose, but he was himself fatally stabbed with a knife by
Cayetano. Cordona had enough strength left to run to the
Mission, where he dropped down calling for the priest. Fortunately, Father Basso was at home, and had the wounded
man quickly taken to one of the front rooms. There he
attended Cordona and gave him the Last Sacraments before
the dying man gasped his last breath.

The murderer was arrested at Santa Barbara, but liberated
on the ground of good conduct, as the Indians claimed, only
three months later, on the eve of Easter Sunday. Cayetano
boldly returned to Santa Inés Mission that same evening, and
even attended Holy Mass next day. The inaction of the police

authorities, however, incensed the Mission Indians to such a degree that they resolved to administer punishment themselves. When, therefore, Cayetano on Easter Sunday started out for his lodgings a Mexican named García waylaid and killed him about six hundred yards from the Mission on the road to the town of Santa Inés. Father Basso would not permit the body to be taken to the Mission cemetery. It was accordingly interred on the Janin Place.

José, the first victim of Cayetano's fury must also have been a wild character, although the husband of the neophyte Salvadora Quinajid. At all events, Father Basso refused Christian burial to the body. The remains were therefore buried under an oaktree which stood near the highway that passes the Donohue estate, but on Mission property near its limits. This tree became a noted landmark which for many years reminded passers-by of the sad tragedy. Later on, during Father Buckler's administration, the tree was cut down and turned into needed firewood.

Long before this period, and especially toward the close of the Nineteenth Century, it had become clear to every friend of the red man that the Indian race in Southern California was fast approaching extinction. In order to avert such a disgrace to the State and to the Government of the United States, Congress was persuaded and the United States Government at last determined to set apart lands for the surviving tribes, on which they could maintain themselves without fear of again being driven away by white greed. By the year 1917, twenty-eight reservations had been assigned to the Indians in Southern California. The majority of these Indians are descendants of the converts who once belonged to the various Missions established by the Franciscan missionaries. As finally patented to the respective Indian tribes, and adduced in the Report of the Indian Commission for the year 1919, the acreage for the smallest reservation, that of Santa Inés, amounts to one hundred and twenty acres of good land with plenty of water.[1] These Indians still attend divine services at the Mission church of their forefathers.

During all the years since the Franciscans surrendered Mission Santa Inés to the Picpus Fathers, little was done to keep the buildings in repair. The income was small and precluded any but the most necessary efforts to arrest decay. An accident, which happened during Father Basso's term, shows how far even at that period decay had proceeded in the very church edifice itself.

On a Rosary Sunday (first Sunday in October) Father Basso celebrated the Holy Mass for the congregation, and after the Gospel ascended the pulpit to preach the sermon on the Rosary. While speaking the pulpit was wrenched off its moorings in the wall, and dropped to the floor. Fortunately the pulpit did not turn over, but came straight down, so that the frightened preacher found himself on the steps of the sanctuary without having suffered more than a strong shock, which made him tremble all through the sacred ceremonies that followed.

The pulpit was never replaced. The Mission church at Santa Inés, therefore, lacks the prominent feature found in all the early Mission churches, no matter how small, as in the case of Purisima Concepcion, where Holy Mass was celebrated in a long narrow apartment. The pulpit was there, but access to it would be through the wall from the vestry.

The little incident will add emphasis to what follows. Our informant, Miss Katharine Donohue, relates: "Father Michael Lynch had written us to come and live at the Old Mission. We were told by those who had come to the valley, a couple of years previously, that they, too, could have lived in the Mission, but that the building was dangerous, the roof was leaky, and the walls around were crumbling. We came in November, 1882. It was a dry year, and so the place wasn't tested for us that year. All the arches were standing and the walls enclosing that space where the frame hall portion is now.

---

[1] See our "*Mission San Luis Rey*," pp. 252, 254.

MR. DONOHOUE'S BLACKSMITH SHOP AND TOOL ROOM. THE CHURCH

We could see that they had been damaged by former storms, and the wall between the dwelling (of front wing) and the church was pretty well washed out, and small slides in it. There was a gap in the roof where it joined the wall of the church, and during the heavy rains of 1884, *when sixty inches of rain fell,* water poured in like a river. My father lost no time in repairing that place. A considerable portion of the wall had crumbled. There was an old stairway (to the organ *loft*) in that room. Water from other parts of the leaky roof would run down there. My father did his best to prevent this, as he did not want to remove the stairway without permission, and the thatched roof overlaid with tiles was hard to work on.

"In the spring of 1884, Father Lynch came to reside at the Mission. He had generally stayed at the College; but some changes were made in the management when he was told that the Mission was where he was supposed to dwell. He occupied the three rooms next to the church. One was where the old stairway entered. He awoke one morning to find the floors covered with water. He then had my father remove the stairway, and close up the opening. My father plastered the walls and filled the washed out parts with adobes. Then Father Lynch got into communication with the Bishop, and the year following a new roof was put on by my father and brothers. After the thatched part had been removed, sheeting and shakes were put on. The tiles were all placed very carefully on the ground.

"My father was a carpenter and stone mason.[2] Being very industrious he fixed up a mortar bed, and up to the time we left was always doing some repairing around the Mission. I remember when the far arches fell during the winter of 1884. Several of the walls around, especially where the frame portion is now, also fell down. There were four sisters younger than myself. My mother, being busy with the housework, would warn me to look out for the little ones, and to keep them away from that part of the front building. The other walls, when

---

[2] As the engraving reveals, Mr. Donohue was also a blacksmith.

we left in 1898, were in good condition. The Fathers Lynch and Farrelly liked things left as they were originally. There was no flooring of any kind in the corridor. I know my father used to tell Father Farrelly that a fence should be built to protect the pillars, as the people who came to church, tied their horses to the pillars and the ropes would in time saw the pillars in two; but Father Farrelly said the people would not feel welcome if they were fenced out. Neither was fencing the backyard approved. Both Fathers wanted the parishioners to drive right in anywhere. When Father Lack came he realized how necessary it was to have a fence. My father then built the fences at his own expense. He also laid a very durable wooden floor in the front corridor, and a brick floor in the rear corridor. A couple of years before we moved out, he put floors in the three rooms occupied by the priests and in the big living room (the ancient *sala* or reception room). The floors are still in good condition.

"We had no way of obtaining water except by hauling it from the river. We did this for seven years, as old timers told us that water could not be found on the *mesa*. Anyway, my brother James thought he would take a chance. So a well digger was hired and with pick and shovel they worked until they found an ample supply of water at a depth of eighty feet. My father purchased a tank and windmill. We then had plenty of water handy. This put an end to the drudgery of hauling a barrel full from the river.

"Father Farrelly had the church roof repaired, but it took some time to collect the required amount from the people of the valley. New panes were put in the windows, because a great many were broken. Owls would be flying in and out and this worried Old Rafael. He told us that before our time campers would chase the owls, and once even climbed up to the windows. From there they shot an owl which had settled down on the head of the statue of Santa Inés. They killed the owl, but also filled the face and breast of the image with shot. The damage was discovered when together with other Indians

Rafael took down the statue for the purpose of cleaning it. New robes were then put on.

"Old Rafael was an aged Indian who took care of the church. Father Lynch had entrusted to him the keys of the church. Twice a week Rafael would come over to the Mission and inspect everything within and the vestry also. Once in a while he would take the vestments out and give them an airing. Before the Sunday on which holy Mass was celebrated, Rafael with other Indians would sweep and clean the church and vestry. On feastdays, such as All Souls' Day, Easter, Corpus Christi and Christmas, he and his helpers would camp nearby. Fernandito would supervise the work. They had draperies and would decorate every altar and picture. On Holy Saturday the main altar would be gorgeously decorated. Then a black cloth would be drawn before the altar hiding it entirely. At the Gloria all the bells were set ringing and the black curtain was withdrawn. The whole ceremony made a deep impression, especially upon the Indians.

"Rafael and Fernandito used to sing the Gregorian Chant when there was a High Mass, which was not often. Rafael had a deep bass voice, whereas Fernandito would sing a high tone. They sang without instrumental accompaniment. Old Margarita, an Indian woman, would occasionally sing along with them. They sang in the body of the church, because the men had to help the priest at Divine Service and even serve at Holy Mass, for want of a server. When Father Lack came, Rafael was unable to serve or sing any more. Miss Lack, my sister, and others would always be singing hymns during the holy Masses.

"After Father Lynch came to live at the Mission, the keys of the church were turned over to us. Rafael would then receive the keys and look after the needs of the church as before. The priests would occasionally give him some amount of money in recognition for his services and for his need.

"My Father was always very careful about everything around the building. Nothing was ever carried away or misused. Before Father Lynch came to live at the Mission, one

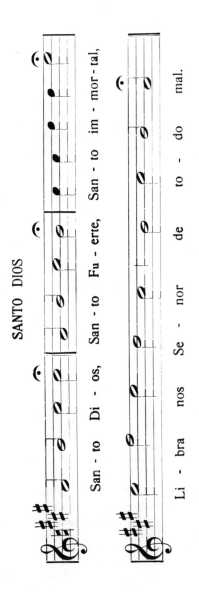

SANTO DIOS

of the three rooms was used as a library, where many books covered the shelves. Father Lynch left the key with my father, and gave him strict orders not to allow any one to enter under any consideration. One day a couple of gentlemen came and said they wanted to go to the library. My father replied: "I have no authority to let anyone into the library."—"Oh!" one of the two said, "but this is Bishop Mora, and we have seen Father Lynch." They had come to remove the books to the Bishop's house at Los Angeles.[3]

"Father Lynch and Father Farrelly were very much more interested in the spiritual welfare of the Indians and others than they were in Mission buildings. If Father Lynch heard that his parishioners were neglecting their religious duties, and he somehow would know about it, he would never wait to call them to an account. The morals of the Zanja Cota (now U. S. Indian Reservation) especially worried him.

"Father Farrelly and Father Lack attended Santa Inés Mission, Lompoc and Sisquoc. The people of Los Alamos would go to the Mission for holy Mass every third Sunday. There were never two holy Masses on any one Sunday. There were no afternoon Services or Benediction.

"Catechism instruction was given at the town of Santa Inés by some ladies, because most of the children lived thereabouts. The priest would take a share in the instruction when it was his Sunday at the Mission. The First holy Communion and Confirmation classes would receive their instructions at the Mission church.

"Father Lynch had two horses—a saddle horse and a horse for the buggy. He left the saddle horse at the Mission to be used in case of sick calls, and to ride where it was impossible to go in a buggy. The animal was very fleet, and was called

---

[3] The collection consisted of theological and philosophical works mainly. There were many sermon and ascetical books in Spanish, and such as are used in any Catholic library, which had been brought there by the early Franciscan Fathers. All were taken to the Bishop's house adjoining the cathedral where we saw them on the shelves.

Chapuli, the Spanish for grasshopper. The horse was also a good swimmer, just the right creature when there were no bridges."

"Father Farrelly was a young man of twenty-seven years, and a great lover of horses of which he had three. As the Father remained at the Mission, only going to his other stations on Saturday afternoon or Sunday morning, it took considerable feed to keep the horses in trim. Twelve tons of hay was not sufficient for a year; but our extensive farming on other lands supplied the rest.

"Father Lack had one horse. As he had little experience with horses, my brothers would take him Saturday evening or Sunday morning to the different places where he was to celebrate holy Mass. The people would come for the priest in case of a sick call, but the Father would always go in his own rig, in order to spare the people the hardship of another trip when the distance was great. One rainy night, however, two men riding one horse arrived about midnight. Their conveyance had broken down. They called the priest to attend a sick person in the vicinity of Los Alamos. My brother James brought out our team and took the Father over. When they returned I heard them saying that on their arrival at the house the sick person was up preparing breakfast.

"Father Lack was a great lover of flowers and plants. He accordingly erected some hothouses, in the rear of the lot or courtyard, and put up a high board wall on the outside for their security. This wall was also a windbreak, for the wind from that direction was very heavy."

We were fortunate to secure the preceding information about a most obscure period in the life of Mission Santa Inés from a lady who had with her family lived in the Mission building for sixteen years. Miss Katharine Donohue related the facts faithfully and intelligently. For this we thank her sincerely in the name of historical truth.

Mr. Thomas Donohue and his sons made many repairs, but for lack of means no radical improvements could be effected. The south end of the monastery already resembled a structure demolished by an earthquake or destroyed by a flood, the haunt of all sorts of creeping creatures from serpents to fleas. A thorough restoration had to be inaugurated or the Mission was doomed.

In this state we saw the once lovely missionary establishment, when early on February 4, 1904, we visited the place for the first time, as we began here our tour through the California Missions in search of historical material for our history of the Franciscan Missions. The Rev. Thomas King, then in charge, was just preparing the chalice for the celebration of holy Mass. We followed his Reverence at the same altar half an hour later. On returning to the reception room, Father King and his all around man John Mullinary welcomed us cheerfully. Then for four days we enjoyed the hospitality of his Reverence and the substantial cookery of Mullinary. Meanwhile we studied the Missions Registers of both Mission Santa Inés and Mission Purisima Concepcion. They were complete and bound in the familiar flexible leather covers. On Sexagesima Sunday, February 7th, we celebrated holy Mass early. During the late Mass offered up by Father King, at his invitation we preached in English and for the sake of the Indians and Mexicans present attempted a suitable instruction in Spanish. In the afternoon we became acquainted with Fernando Cardinas, better known as Fernandito for his short stature, who showed us everything of note and acquainted us with many historical facts which no one else knew so well on account of his fifty years intercourse with the Mission Indians of that region.

Four months later, Rt. Rev. Thomas James Conaty, D. D., the Bishop of the Diocese of Los Angeles, appointed the Rev. Alexander Buckler pastor of Mission Santa Inés and the outlying stations Lompoc and Sisquoc together with the surviving Indians. He was also ordered to restore the venerable Mission buildings. It was high time for such a move. The preceding year had happened to be a dry one. Up to the time of our visit in February no rain had fallen in nine months. A wet season would spell the ruin of the Convento part. Father Buckler proved the right man for the task. With truly Bavarian tenacity he examined every nook and corner of the church and of the surviving front wing or monastery. Then he made his plans accordingly. An incident added fuel to his determination. One morning he entered the church and went to the sanctuary. As he approached the altar, to his amazement and indignation he discovered a snake, about four feet long, stretched out at full length on the white altar cloth before the tabernacle. He speedily knocked it down and killed it. As the sacristy or end of the church edifice is located on the opposite side of the courtyard and ruined portion of the monastery, it appeared clear that the whole group of buildings was infested with the loathsome creatures.

The condition of the vestments convinced Father Buckler that he could not singlehanded cope with the difficulties encountered. Feminine hands, directed by a capable head and a stout heart devoid of all thought of self would be needed, not merely for housekeeping but as an assistant in the general restoration. Where could such a person be found? He resolved to appeal to his niece in far away Minnesota. He was asking a great sacrifice, indeed. The young woman would have to renounce all worldly prospects, and bury herself in the solitude of the old Mission structures, and think of nothing but work, work! The nearest and only neighbors would be the Donohue family, a quarter of a mile away. The village of Solvang had not as yet been thought of. There was dearth of almost everything, yet no store nearer than the town of Santa Inés four miles distant. The Father described the situation and left the decision to the niece, Miss Mary Goulet, who promptly and heroically consented to leave her home in order to assist her uncle in the great undertaking.

The cheerful news from his generous niece put Father Buckler into a happy mood which he communicated to us in the following letter.

"Santa Inés Mission, California, August 31, 1904.—Dear Rev. Father,—How I enjoyed your missive! Gladly do I

VARIOUS VIEWS OF THE MISSION.

place myself at your service. You are welcome at any time. Unfortunately, there are so many question marks in the way so that it is proper to explain to you the whole condition of things here. I arrived at the Mission on July 22nd, and encountered solitude, ruin and abomination of desolation everywhere. A disagreeable old Methodist couple occupies a portion of the house, and it is very difficult to induce them to move out. However, by October the first they will leave. Not till then can I begin to live.

"Dirt and neglect stare at me all around. There is a lack of linens, kitchen utensils, etc. My housekeeper, my niece, will appear on October 1st. Then we shall start in to clean out the house, purify the interior of the church, and procure the articles necessary for housekeeping.

"I am therefore compelled to postpone the celebration of the centennial of the Mission founding. It is absolutely impossible to arrange any celebration by September 17th, the date of the founding. There are no funds on hand anyway. At all events, I have thought of waiting till September 17, 1905.

"After November 1st, Rev. Father, you may come at any time, because by that date I hope to be in a position to harbor a priest. As it is, I am a sort of hermit, and as a Tertiary of St. Francis, half a Franciscan also.—Your devoted Alexander Buckler."

During those early years the new pastor of Mission Santa Inés led a lonely life, indeed. "He was born and reared amidst refinement," Miss Goulet, whose description will follow presently, informs us, "and he was such a finished musician! Here he was buried, so to speak, as far as his talents were concerned. And how keenly he felt not having a piano! At one time he bought a cheap violin, thinking with it to partly satisfy the longing; but with building fences, mixing adobe mud, and the many other manual labors that called for his attention, he found the fingers had lost their nimbleness, and

REV. ALEXANDER BUCKLER.

would not respond well to the touch of the violin strings. So, in despair, he finally gave it to an Indian who occasionally served at holy Mass."

At the urgent request of Father Buckler, we interrupted our journey in search of historical material at Los Angeles, and hastened to help him out among the Spanish-speaking parishioners. We took the stage at Gaviota on Saturday, November 19, 1904, nine months after our first visit, and arrived at Mission Santa Inés in the afternoon. We were cordially welcomed by his Reverence. At the same time he introduced his all around assistant, Miss Mary L. Goulet, who had arrived on September 21st. "Can this comely but frail-looking young lady be equal to the difficulties she will encounter?", was our mental comment. In less than a week this maiden of twenty-three years had proved her mettle. After that we had no more misgivings as to her courage and ability. Ere long we found her a well-trained and noble-hearted lady, who went about her duties conscientiously, energetically yet gently, silently yet cheerfully, asking no curious questions, but looking after the needs with solicitude, and having every thing in neat and orderly condition. Truly, the pastor and the Mission of Santa Inés had acquired a jewel.

Next morning, Sunday, November 20th, an odd Sunday for the Mission, and therefore without holy Mass, in Father Buckler's company we started out in an open buggy for one of his two distant stations, named Sisquoc. The other was Lompoc. We arrived at the little church at about ten o'clock. People were already waiting. During Father's Mass, we, ourselves, heard confessions, and then we said holy Mass and preached in Spanish. Thereupon we gave instructions to a dozen grown up girls, while Father baptized. Then we had to drive two miles for breakfast, which was taken at one o'clock p. m. Thereupon Father entertained us and the family with the piano and singing. We passed the night at this hospitable home.

Monday morning early we rode back two miles to the church, where people were already waiting for the opportunity

Old Mission Santa Inés, Founded 1804.

VIEWS OF MISSION CORRIDOR AT VARIOUS DATES.
JOHN MULLINARY IN REAR CORRIDOR.

of receiving the Sacraments. While Father celebrated holy Mass and later, we ourselves heard thirty-three confessions, and then said holy Mass during which those concerned received Holy Communion. Thereupon we proceeded on the road to the Mission for a mile and a half from the little church to take breakfast at Wickenden's. Thereupon we followed the road to the Mission, which we reached at about one p. m., very much tired out.

Father Buckler wished us to stay till the following Sunday, to hold the Divine Service, because he would have to go to Lompoc, for the same purpose. Meanwhile we rested and studied the Old Records of Baptisms, Marriages and Burials which were complete, as were the same volumes from the ancient Mission of Purisima Concepcion. Numerous notes were the result of our investigation. The contents were utilized in this little volume. We said holy Mass every day, but the church was exceedingly cold despite its thick walls. The rooms in the Mission, except the office, which has a fireplace, are also cold on account the cement floors.

On St. Cecilia's Day, November 22nd, we celebrated the Saint's feast, and Father Buckler entertained the household of three with music from a talking machine and songs of his own which all cheered us greatly.

Sunday 27th of November was an odd Sunday for the Mission, wherefore but few people, possibly fifty all told, attended holy Mass at 10:30.

The weather was cold, and in the rooms, save in the office, there were no heaters. A slight attack of malaria, an old companion of ours, caused Father to insist that I should rest during the week and assist him on Sunday, December 4th, by taking the last holy Mass and preaching both in English and Spanish. We agreed, and during the week again went over the Mission Registers. On Thursday, December 1st, John Mullinary took us in a buggy to the ancient mill reservoir, a wonderful piece of masonry. Then we drove to the former College, and found it going to ruins. At the Mission we became acquainted with the Rev. Father Lack of Arroyo Grande, who had been in charge here for 13 years. Sunday passed as planned. On Monday we left for ruined Mission Purisima Concepcion.

We have personally and thoroughly investigated the situation at Old Mission Santa Inés; we have searched the Mission Registers, and have taken notes on the spot of all that had transpired there down to the day of our visit. At the same time we have also had a taste of the missionary activities and difficulties faced by the respective pastors and related in this volume. What happened thereafter we have asked faithful Miss Goulet to report in her own way. This most interesting narrative is contained in the following chapter.

CHAPTER XII.

"Dear Rev. Father,—I will try to give you in my own simple words the information you desire, in order to show clearly how very badly neglected and dilapidated the Mission was when Father Buckler and I came there, and what was done during the early years of its restoration. You, dear Father, know something of its condition at that time, for you visited there before and after our arrival.

"Vandals must have entered the buildings when no one was around, and then played havoc with what was in reach. At any rate, no one who visits the Mission today for the first time can conceive of the appalling condition it was in at that time.

"Numberless priceless as well as common articles were unearthed. For instance, we found the beautiful old oil painting of St. Francis in the old tank house under the water tank, a dark and damp place full of debris. It was without frame, crumpled up, and partly buried in the soil. As proof of it, you can see the painting at the Mission this day, with the bottom portion cut off, thus cutting off the feet of the picture of the Saint. I tried to save it, but it was so decayed that it fairly dropped off when I put it in the present frame.

"Another instance was the finding of one of three pewter containers, which, I discovered later, was one of a set that belonged in a lovely leather covered box. That was unearthed when we were doing some gardening in the backyard. Not till this third container was discovered, did I connect it with the leather covered box. When I called Father's attention to it, he at once recognized it as the Holy Oil stocks and box. Unfortunately the box has a hole cut into its cover. It had been used as a poor box. John Mullinary told us that it was done during Father King's time."

"Other treasures unearthed while we were there, were the three altar stones, buried in the cemetery, and so long that no one knew or remembered where. James Donohue, having heard about the altar stones, tried to locate them, but failed. However, with Father's persistence, and the help of an occasional tramp to do the digging, they were finally brought to light.

"Thus it came to pass that one thing after another was discovered, cleaned, and restored to its place.

"Then there were the vestments. Oh, the beautiful, but dilapidated, frayed, ragged vestments! They were my despair, but later my great pride and joy. Young as I was, and inexperienced too, I loved beautiful materials, and it hurt me to see all those beautiful old fabrics in such disrepair, and those lovely old linens in such shameful condition! The whole mess of them shoved into the big drawers of the lovely old chests in the sacristy! No order, or system whatsoever.

"I spent many a Sunday after my arrival, before I got things straightened out in such a way that Father could have a whole set of vestments in one color. Some of them had parts missing, and others had parts so ragged that they could not be worn. Many a Sunday, too, before I could do more than to cut the rags that hung from them, or put in a stitch or two, here and there, to hold them together till I had more time, as so many things were demanding my attention during those trying days.

"Those beautiful brocades, centuries old; all hand loomed; almost too sacred to touch. What a privilege to be able to repair them, and to restore to their former use, in the service of holy Mass!

"The linens, too, all hand loomed, and beautifully made up by some loving hands, with stitches so fine that they could not be seen with the naked eye; but so neglected, so soiled, and in much need of repair!

"It was a huge task, and so little time with the hundred and one other duties. Five years elapsed before the last vestment was finished, suspended from its hanger, and placed in the

RESTORED SPANISH VESTMENTS. VESTMENT CASE.

vestments case with its companions; and the last piece of linen repaired, ironed out and laid away in the same huge drawer of the same lovely chest that held them when in such disrepair.

"Father loved the old things, and I loved caring for them, and every thing used in the services of the church during our time.

"After I had finished making over and mending the vestments, there was left a lot of various colors, too small to be of use. Father asked me if I could patch them together, dye them black, and make a vestment with stole and maniple of them in which he could be buried. I did that, using whatever colored pieces there were. I dipped the whole in black dye. When we came to Santa Barbara, Father took it along, and when he had passed away, the body was laid in that black vestment.

"As near as I can remember, when all were repaired—there were two red, one purple, one black, one green, and two white copes;—three white, two red, two green, two purple, two black and two rose-colored vestments.

"There were also repaired and restored one purple, one black, one red, one green and two white frontals or antipendiums.

"With regard to the work of restoration begun by Father Buckler by order of Bishop Conaty with the year 1905, I will touch only the most important points, and give them as well as I remember.

"In March, 1905, we had a terrific rain storm which destroyed the wind-mill. It blew the wheel and fan tail completely off and landed the pieces in the field. It also tore away great portions from the Convento roof and threw them into the adjoining field yards away.

"The roof at that time was covered with "shakes" by the Donohue boys, the Bishop paying the cost of the material."

"The well was dug by hand. It was four feet square and ninety feet deep lined with boards all the way down. During the course of time the lumber decayed. Then a circular curb-ing of wood was put inside the old square one, and the wind-mill erected.

"The destruction of parts of the roof caused us much incon-venience during the remainder of the rainy season, but the loss of the windmill was a greater drawback, because we had to haul water for household purposes from the Santa Inés River. John Mullinary, who at that time was at the Mission made a sled. On this he placed a barrel. He had this primitive conveyance drawn to the river by a horse every morning, filled the barrel with water and returned to the Mission over a rough road. When he arrived the barrel was usually but one-third full of water.

"We worried along for some time. The Father placed his difficulties before good Bishop Conaty, who instructed Father Buckler to have the well and mill repaired, the "shakes" on the roof replaced with shingles, and to send the bills to the Diocesan Chancery. Accordingly, Father had a new mill erected, and an eight or ten inch terra cotta pipe put down in the old circular casing. We had water enough once more."

"A new shingle roof was put on the Convento part of the Mission so far as there were habitable rooms which portion was a little more than half of the Convento as it is now. The cost of the well, wind mill, and roofing amounted to $2,606.27, which was paid by the Bishop.

"From that time on, Father and I, with the help of the occasional tramp or wayfarer, who were few at that period, built chicken houses, fences, cleaned up old wooden structures, tore away ruined portions of tumbled down adobes, repaired broken windows, battered doors, patched up crumbling adobe holes here and there and everywhere in the walls, filled up holes in the asphalt floors and covered them with concrete to prevent rats, snakes and other unwelcome inhabitants of the place from coming up through the apertures, until it seemed there would be no end to the task.

"In the meantime we set all sorts of traps for skunks, weasles, gophers, rats, and mice. We would be shooting hawks,

1. REAR VIEW OF HOBO VILLA. 2. TOWER AFTER EARTHQUAKE, MARCH 7, 1911. 3. TRAMP TAKING A MEAL. 4. VISITORS FROM SANTA BARBARA. 5. A VICIOUS REPTILE.

owls, woodpeckers and ground squirrels, and catching and killing all kinds of snakes, such as the corral, the red racer, water, garter and gopher snakes. In addition we would be forever bumping up against horned toads, common toads, tarantulas, centipedes, *wicos*, *mata enadós*, and last, but not least, innumerable fleas.

"As to snakes in particular, I have never tried to put their story into print, although I have on a number of occasions put them into bottles, and covered them with alcohol. My first recollection of one was an afternoon when I went to the dining room. The sun was casting its beams through the windows on the deep recesses of the adobe walls. There stretched out at full length, about four feet, in one of the recesses was this impudent snake taking a sun bath. It did not move as I came quite near to take a closer look, and make sure that I was not mistaken, or walking in my sleep. I ran for the broom, gave it a few little "pushes." It then crawled away through a broken window pane, dropped on the ground outside in the corridor, and disappeared in some debris near by. Shortly afterwards, on opening the kitchen sink one of those pesky things noiselessly crawled out. Thereafter I always kept a hoe near the kitchen door as a weapon to kill the intruders. If they were small ones, I had a fruit jar handy. I would place a broom on them, and the jar in such a position that as they tried to get away from the broom, they found themselves in the fruit jar. Then it was easy to fill the jar with alcohol, and later transfer them to smaller containers. At one time we had about thirty specimens of all sorts of reptiles in bottles.

"On one occasion Father Buckler, late in the night before retiring, wanted to have a drink of water in the kitchen. As he came along, candle in hand, he just missed stepping on a corral snake with his bare feet. It was coiled in the middle of the asphalt floor in the hall leading to the kitchen. He killed it with a hoe; but never again would he go in his bare feet, or without bearing a light.

"A gopher snake is not considered poisonous; but the corral is said to be very much so at certain periods of the year. Furthermore, the gopher snake is not always easy to see or discover, because it is the color of dry grass. The corral is usually easier to detect, for it is black and white, or black and almost yellow. The stripes alternating round its body." See accompaning sketch.

"The reptiles would appear occasionally as late as 1918 or thereabouts. People told us not to kill them as they would eat the gophers; but we always did kill them. They may have been alright in the fields, but we did not care to have them share the Mission with us. I remember one of them that had practised remarkable stunts, and they were not afraid to show off. I had been out in the garden in front of the Convento. On turning upwards I saw the head of a snake dangling from the tin gutter under the roof in the middle of the arch, just over the front entrance. I called Father to bring his gun, which he always had ready for such emergencies, and he shot it in the head. It wriggled awhile and then came tumbling down on the cement walk. It must have reached the gutter by means of a rosebush. It was spring time, and so many linnets nesting in the rosebush and in the very gutters. It is likely that the serpent was in search of bird eggs. Anyhow, it was a long time before serpents and kindred inhabitants of the old haunts had been driven out of the buildings.

"Those were busy and full days. There was scarcely time to prepare the meals, which, by the way, were cooked on an old cast iron stove, set up under one of the arches of the rear corridor, and often flavored with smoke when the wind blew in the wrong direction, or the stove refused to draw; but, what matter, we were working hard and appetites were good.

"Four of the large rooms were divided into two so as to make them more convenient and home-like. Father hired a Frenchman from Santa Inés town by the name of La Fontaine, (who claimed to be a carpenter) to help him put up these division walls; but when they had the two by four timbers up, he announced that he could not do the lathing, and left the job.

"For some months we walked around these two by four timbers in the middle of these rooms, till one Saturday morning, when Father was leaving for Lompoc to be away till the following Monday, I got the bright idea that I might do some lathing myself. So when Father had disappeared, I got busy with hammer, nails and a step-ladder. I lathed one whole side of one wall eighteen feet wide and fourteen feet high. From that time on, all of my precious spare moments were spent going up and down the ladder to nail on laths, until all of the four walls were finished on both sides of their eighteen by fourteen sides.

"Sometime later, Thomas Donohue took compassion on us and offered to do the plastering. He was not exactly a plasterer, but all the better, for his work was rough and rather resembled the adobe walls.

"Not till the year 1911, when the big work of the restoration was done, did these walls get finished, that is to say, the door frames put in, the doors hung, and the mop board put in place. Then again I had to do my bit, and painted all the new wood work, and the old to harmonize, in all of these rooms. With the help of a tramp, a young fellow of twenty-three years, a lithographer by trade, and Arthur Hendess by name, I whitewashed nine rooms. The young fellow did the ceilings, while I did the walls.

"These, dear good Father, are a few of the high lights that made the Santa Inés Mission a habitable and cosy place to live in, and built in our hearts such a warm fire of love for every thing about it.

"In the year 1911, in the month of March (I have forgotten the date and do not find it any where) the bell tower fell, and three of the huge buttresses on the cemetery side of the church, and the one supporting the last arch of the Convento part in the front.

"Then it was that Bishop Conaty of blessed memory came to Father's assistance, and at this time also the Native Sons of the Golden West. I cannot say definitely how much the Bishop contributed at this time, but believe it was $6,000, notwithstanding the reports of other figures. The Native Sons contributed $900 towards the rebuilding of the bell tower.

"This big job of restoration was given to Magnus Johnson, a contractor of Santa Barbara. The contract called for the rebuilding of the bell tower and buttresses, the taking down of the tile of the church, and putting on a board and tar paper roofing, then replacing the tile, and placing a concrete foundation along the Cemetery side of the church to keep it from further decay from the winter rains, and putting on gutters all around the church and Convento roofs. The contract also included the reconstruction of the south end of the Convento which was down and had become the haunt of reptiles, etc. The cleaning out of the place, amounting to about one-third of the Convento or front wing, was mostly done by the tramps who lodged in the rear for some days or longer.

"It was Father's wish to have the tile, which had been on the Convento part of the Mission, but for many years lying scattered around, put back on the roof. He also wanted a cistern put in the back yard and have the water from the roofs run into it. Furthermore, the reservoir in front of the Mission was to be re-surfaced in concrete and roofed over to catch the water from the front part of the Mission; but the Bishop did not think it was absolutely necessary at the time and asked Father to wait a while.

"Father knowing how expensive it was to bring all the tools and machinery from Santa Barbara to do the work a second time, and how difficult it would be to hunt up workmen again, was rather disappointed. Undaunted, however, and feeling that it would be such a saving to have all this work done while the paraphernalia was on the ground, he took up the matter with the contractor, Mr. Johnson, and came to some agreement, whereby he could pay it off at his own convenience.

"So it was that the concrete floors were laid under both front and back arches of the Convento, the cistern in the back garden built and the reservoir in the front re-surfaced and covered over with a corrigated roofing. Father paid for this part of the restoration from his own private fund as his contribution towards the Mission.

"As for laying the tile on the Convento part, Mr. Johnson agreed to donate a half day's work of his men towards that, and Father appealed to the Danish people of the new settlement of Solvang,[1] as a matter of civic pride, to lend assistance, which they did. So one morning came nine or ten men, who with the force at hand gathered all the usable tile that were scattered about the place and covered all of the front part of the roof and a portion of the roof in the back. While I busied myself cooking a sumptuous meal for generous appetites. The bills for that portion which Father donated are in my possession, the rest of the bills were perhaps left at the Mission."

"It was not all clear sailing for Father with his great work, however. When it became known that good Bishop Conaty was lending a hand and ready to help, an enterprising busybody came to Father and wanted him to turn over the work of supervising the re-construction to him. Father refused to do so. This seemed to greatly displease this man, and after going about creating dissension among Father's people and others, he went to Los Angeles to see the Bishop about it, but failed to get an audience, as the enclosed letter of the Bishop to Father clearly shows.

---

[1] Colony of Lutheran Danes transplanted from Texas to the vicinity of Mission Santa Inés. The relations between the newcomers and the Mission have been amicable from the start. The present head, at our request, explained as follows: "The Danish Colony-*Solvang*-Sunny Vale— was founded in 1911 by the two ministers Benedict Nordentoft and J. M. Gregersen, Prof. P. P. Hornsyld, Lawrence Petersen and Mads Freese. When Mads Freese first arrived there was only the Mission; since then more than one hundred homes have been built. Atterdag College, a Folk High School, was erected in 1914. The purpose of this institution is to broaden the horizon of young men and women culturally and spiritually, rather than give academic training. The present leader is Rev. Marius Krog."

MOST REVEREND THOMAS JAMES CONATY, D. D.

Chancery Office,
114 East Second Street, Los Angeles,
April 15, 1911.

"Rev. A. Buckler,
    Santa Ynez, Cal.

My Dear Father Buckler:—

Mr. E—[2] called here last night with reference to the Santa Ynez Mission rebuilding, seeking authority to have him rebuild it. I did not see him as he came while I was engaged in other business, and I understand he went home today. Had I seen him I would have referred him to you because all that relates to the Mission rebuilding I wish to place in your hands. If they wish to help us in the work we will be very much pleased, but it is our intention to have it all placed in your hands.

With best wishes for the Easter time, I am yours very sincerely,

Thomas J. Conaty."

"When the work was well under way, this man learned of Father's intention of putting tile on the Convento roof, he made himself obnoxious again, going about among the workmen. He did his best to persuade them and the contractor that the beams under the roof of the Convento were too decayed and weak to stand the weight of the heavy tile. Failing to impress them, he wrote to the Bishop. The Bishop in turn sent his letter to Father, and added that Father should use his own discretion in the matter. I remember clearly of seeing this letter, but fail to find it among Father's papers here. Father halted the work long enough to secure an expert from Santa Barbara to come up to examine and test the beams. It meant an added expense, but it settled the question. The expert not only found that the beams were sufficiently strong, but pronounced them far superior to any new timbers that they could put in their place. And so the tile was laid and adorns the Convento to this day.

---

[2] Name suppressed for the sake of the family.

"Now, dear Padre, it would seem that the story of the restoration could not be complete without saying something about, what Father called his "Dick Turpins," the tramps, the hobos, or wayfarers. We really had quite a number of them considering the times.

"All of the work done by the tramps was very slow, and sometimes very aggravating. These tramps were of all sorts, of all nationalities, each with his peculiarities and traits, and often had to be humored a lot in order to get much work out of them. If they only wanted one meal, or a meal and lodging for the night, they would not do very much work in return, and often do nothing, especially the older men or the crippled. But should they stay a week or two, or a month or more, as sometimes would happen in the rainy seasons, then they would accomplish quite a bit of work, depending on the willingness of the man.

"If they staid more than a day or so and worked, Father gave them some money, depending on the ability of the man, the kind of work to be done, or on how rich he felt at the time. Some times he gave them a dollar a day, and at other times, five dollars a week, and sometimes only ten dollars a month, especially during the rainy season when there were so many days that it was impossible to work in adobe, do any digging, or such like work.

"In return for meals, and lodgings, Father would have them do little jobs, such as cleaning out debris, chopping and carrying wood, hoeing weeds, hauling away decayed adobes, and many other things that were constantly to be done. After the big re-construction, they helped a lot in cleaning up, leveling the huge pile of debris left by the fallen bell tower and buttresses.

"Of course, many of them were not anxious to work, and did little or nothing, and many of them were too old to do anything. Also a few were so desperate looking that we just gave them a meal and sent them on their way. Others were anxious to work; some wanted a little money; others were willing to work for their keep, especially during the rainy seasons, and some would remain a number of weeks. Father always kept smoking and chewing tobacco on hand for those who used it, as he found a man was happier with it, and worked better, too.

"I have here what Father called his "Hobo Register" where he entered the number that came, their names if he learned them, their trades if they had any, and then his own private remarks about them. It was started on November 26th, 1907 and continued till the year 1922 in July.

"In that first year of November and December there were only four entries made, but the following year, 1908 there were entered 114 men and 352 meals handed out to them and so on through the years. The peak seems to have been reached in the year 1912 when we gave out 619 meals and in 1913 when we gave out 462 meals.

"The food that we gave out consisted mostly of beans, bread and coffee and what ever vegetables or other thing I happened to have on hand, perhaps cottage cheese or a glass of milk, as we had our own cow at that time. Always, when the rainy season came on I would put the bean pot on the stove, and kept it going till the warm days of spring, when the gardens began to give out their fruits, and the tramp could help himself along his way. He usually preferred to do his own cooking, under a bridge, or the shade of an oak tree by the way side.

"In building the wooden structures in the back of the Mission, we arranged to have two rooms for these wayfarers, or tramps, and called it the Hobo Villa. There were two beds in each room and sometimes they were filled to capacity with others, rolled up in their blankets, sleeping on the floor.

"I am enclosing a little picture which shows the back view of this row of rooms, used for work-shop, garage, and chicken houses, besides the "Hobo Villa." You will notice that there are plenty of windows in it. They are the windows taken from the old hot-house built during Father Lack's time. Father made use of them here, also all the windows in the new part of the Convento were from this hot-house.

"This long wooden building has only a slanting roof sloping towards the front and the Convento. Father put it up as a protection against the heavy winds that used to come from that direction when the country was all open through the valley, and before the Danish settlement came into existence.

PLAN OF MISSION SANTA INEZ, AS RECONSTRUCTED BY REV. A. BUCKLER

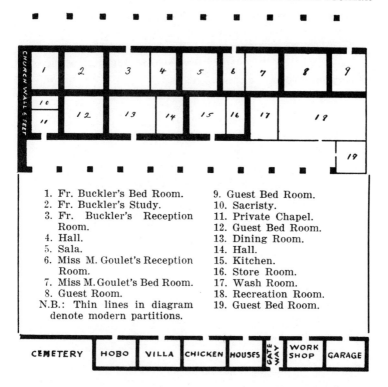

1. Fr. Buckler's Bed Room.
2. Fr. Buckler's Study.
3. Fr. Buckler's Reception Room.
4. Hall.
5. Sala.
6. Miss M. Goulet's Reception Room.
7. Miss M. Goulet's Bed Room.
8. Guest Room.
N.B.: Thin lines in diagram denote modern partitions.

9. Guest Bed Room.
10. Sacristy.
11. Private Chapel.
12. Guest Bed Room.
13. Dining Room.
14. Hall.
15. Kitchen.
16. Store Room.
17. Wash Room.
18. Recreation Room.
19. Guest Bed Room.

DIAGRAM OF MISSION AS IT IS NOW AND BUILDINGS IN REAR.

DETAILS SUPPLIED BY MISS M. GOULET, RE-DRAWN BY BROTHER SERAPHIN O. F. M.

"Father Lack had a board fence built, as he told us, for the same purpose of breaking the wind. When we had the heavy rain and wind storm of March, 1905 the ground got so water soaked that the wind just blew the whole fence down flat to the ground. To prevent a repetition of that same thing, Father re-built it with a double wall, roofing it over and dividing it into rooms.

"This work was all done by Father and myself with the help of the occasional tramp, without any financial help of the Bishop. I well remember when the rains came on and no tramps made their appearance, I went up on the roof and nailed shingles for three days to complete the job. Then slipping down every evening I was so stiff and crippled from the cramped position, that I could scarcely walk home; but the job got finished, and that is what Father wanted.

"Now dear Rev. Father, you are very kind and most generous in your appreciation of my humble work at the Mission. You have made me feel well repaid for all the hardships, heartaches, disappointments and discouragements that came and went during those long years; but, as I look back, there are many bright spots too.

"Fortunately I had the happy faculty of seeing the bright side of life, and making the best of things as they came along. I would not now take worlds for my stay and experiences in what to me is the dearest and most beautiful of all Missions; and it leaves no regrets.—*Mary Laura Goulet.*"

CHAPTER XIII.

The Year 1911 will be forever memorable in the annals of Mission Santa Inés. The heavy rainfalls in the first months threatened to wipe out the whole group of buildings, so that rumors circulated that both the church and the monastery were doomed. On March 9th, indeed the *Daily Press* one morning cast gloom over the community at Santa Barbara with the headline in prominent letters:—"NO CHANCE TO SAVE SANTA INÉS MISSION." "Telephone reports from Santa Inés received at a late hour last night, state that there is no chance of saving Santa Inés Mission unless the rains abate immediately. A portion of the structure gave way to the undermining waters Tuesday, March 8th, and the remaining walls are fast crumbling away. The destruction of Santa Inés Mission yesterday (March 8) by flood waters marks the passing of the third of the 21 Mission establishments built along the Camino Real by the Franciscan Fathers and extending from San Diego in the south to Sonoma in the North."

This news, on March 14, brought out the following lament in the *Morning Press* of Santa Barbara under the heading in extra large letters: "ANOTHER OF THE OLD MONUMENTS MARKING EL CAMINO REAL ALLOWED TO DISAPPEAR." T. W. Moore of this city, who has lived in Santa Barbara from his boyhood, writes to the *Press* as follows:—

"Who is it that is not moved to a feeling of sympathy when he beholds these works of great men achieved in a time so remote from the present? When it required the most skillful and thoughtful methods to raise these monuments which have endured for centuries and would still endure for many more if some care and attention were bestowed upon them from time to time!

"Such were my feelings when in your paper of Wednesday morning I read of the destruction of the Santa Inés Mission. Born and brought up as I was in Santa Inés, every boyish memory I still cherish of this beautiful valley centers around this dear old landmark. It seems as though my lodestone were still near this sacred spot and every once in a while I would be drawn there to make my visit, although my last visit, which was a little over a year ago was tinged with sadness, for I saw then that unless something were done to protect the Mission against the ravages of winter its destruction would be inevitable. I solicited the aid of the Land Mark society through their foremost worker, Mr. Charles F. Lummis. He wrote me that although they had taken up the matter of the restoration of several of the old landmarks of California, foremost among them being the old Missions, yet he was powerless to lend any aid on the restoration of this Mission as it was in the hands of the Bishop. It is to be regretted that a portion of the revenues derived from the church properties in the Santa Inés valley, which consists of rentals from about 14,000 acres of land, could not have been applied to the preservation of this old monument.

"No more will the bell ring out its sweet-toned notes from the century-old belfry! No more will the laborer in the field be guided as to the time of day by the ringing out of the Angelus bells. All this is past. The century-old monument lies in a heap and her bells are buried in the ruins.

"All too fast is California losing her old landmarks, and even though they be restored they never seem the same—the break is always there."

Four months later, July 26, *The Independent* of Santa Barbara published the following, with heavy headlines:—

"BISHOP WILL RESTORE SANTA INÉS MISSION."

"Grateful to Native Sons, But Cannot Accept Conditions Imposed.

"Rt. Rev. Bishop Conaty is prepared to go ahead and restore historic Santa Inés Mission, damaged by the storm last winter, thus undoubtedly ending the little controversy which has arisen between the church authorities and the Native Sons.

"The Native Sons appropriated a sum towards the restoration of the Mission, but there were certain stipulations which the Church authorities could not accept. There has been correspondence between State Senator L. H. Roseberry and Rt. Rev. Bishop Conaty in the matter.

"The following is the Bishop's letter to Senator Roseberry, just made public, which probably closes the incident:—

"Los Angeles, Cal., June 10, 1911.

My Dear Mr. Roseberry:

"Your letter of June 6, relative to the preservation and restoration of the Santa Inés Mission has been received. I am deeply grateful for the interest taken by the local parlor of the Native Sons, but I cannot accept the conditions under which their co-operation is given.

"In the last seven years I have spent in the neighborhood of $7,000 in restoring that Mission and have already arranged to see to the repairing made necessary by the recent storm. I think you will readily see that I cannot, in justice to myself and to the position which I hold, abdicate in favor of any committee in the work which becomes necessary for any church building.

"You may not be aware of how much has been done for that Mission during the past few years and how little assistance has come from any direction toward it. I am quite certain whatever will be done for it in the future will be done along the best possible lines. For myself, I am thoroughly interested in the maintenance of these landmarks and I am prepared to see to it that the necessary funds be raised for the repairs. I would appreciate any assistance that might be given in the matter, but if the assistance is given subject to the conditions laid down in your letter, I must respectfully decline to accept it.

"One thing is certain, the Santa Inés Mission will be restored and preserved, and I have already in hand money sufficient for the work. I am exceedingly grateful to you for the kindness of your communication and feel that you will appreciate the justice of my position in the matter."

"Bishop Conaty, of blessed memory," Miss Mary Goulet writes us, "was at the Mission on three different occasions during our time there, but not to administer Confirmation. His first visit happened on July 18, 1907; his second visit occured on July 28, 1910; and the last or third visit was on August 3rd, 1911, when he came to see Father Buckler about the restoration of the bell tower and other things that were to be done."

Shortly after, at Lompoc, Bishop Conaty administered the Sacrament of Confirmation to a class of children prepared by Father Buckler then still in charge of Lompoc. At the dinner, which followed the ceremonies, the Bishop took occasion to express his satisfaction at all that had been done in restoring Mission Santa Inés. Among other pleasant words uttered by the Bishop, according to Miss Flora Fabing of Lompoc, were these: *"I am convinced that the very excellent work done at the Mission by Father Buckler is largely due to the help and cooperation of his very efficient niece, Miss Goulet."*

The Knights of Columbus at Los Angeles also heeded the appeal. At a general meeting and public entertainment, March 28, 1911, on motion of Hon. Joseph Scott, it was unanimously voted to begin at once active preparations for an Entertainment to secure funds to aid Bishop Conaty in the restoration of Santa Inés Mission.

The resolution passed enthusiastically after Miss Alice Stevens, a convert, and then energetic editor of *The Tidings*, the Diocesan Weekly, had read a paper entitled *The California Missions in Literature*. We herewith reproduce the paragraphs,

CHURCH BUILDING OF SANTA INES BEING RE-ROOFED.

which, even after twenty-one years, are still pertinent to the history of the Missions in general and of Mission Santa Inés in particular. . . . . .

"While the lofty mountains and fertile valleys of our Golden State have been a source of inspiration to some of the really great writers of the west, whose work will live so long as men love the handiwork of God; and while the mining days, with their attendant hardships, have been portrayed in song and story by virile pens, no theme in the entire west replete with romantic interest, has so gripped the heartstrings and fired the souls of all classes of writers, good, bad and indifferent, as have the old, historic missions of California. Their spirit breathes in our literature, and their influence is impressed upon our western art.

"To the commercial citizen they appeal as a stock in trade to promote business enterprises, and he exploits them as a drawing card for the tourists. He never spoils what he considers a good story for the sake of the truth, but by deviating from the truth he invariably spoils a better story than the best that a distorted fancy possibly could picture. Our book stores are filled with literary junk dealing with the subjects of the missions, purporting to depict life and scenes incident to the days of their greatest glory, written by authors whose sole aim seems to have been to weave a cobweb of fiction around a sacred subject whose character they were utterly incapable of comprehending, in order that they themselves might pose as western writers with the stamp of the dollar mark to measure the merits of their work. Others have even stooped to lower depths of degradation in this line, and utilized the pictures of the old missions for trade marks. What a sacrilege! A law should be enacted prohibiting such desecration.

"There is another kind of writer who, unintentionally, does quite as much harm, and that is the undependable and indefensible enthusiast, who skims along the surface of things, weaves a tale from the fabric of dreams, clothes it in beautiful flowers of rhetoric and sends it out into the world with a message wholly at variance with actual conditions, and yet founded upon just enough fact to give it the semblance of truth. The pens of such writers should be muzzled. They are too superficial to delve deeply into the subject and they impose upon the lack of authentic information of their readers........

"THE SPIRIT THAT PERVADES THE MISSIONS"

"But there is a spirit pervading these missions which eludes commercialism and defies materialism, and unless that spirit rests upon the pen of those that would tell the story or depict the glory of the old missions of California, they will labor in vain, and that is the same spirit which prompted their building, a deeply religious spirit which seeks but the glory of God and the salvation of souls, the spirit of the Catholic Church and its Divine Founder abiding with it."

Miss Stevens spoke of the impossibility of non-Catholic writers grasping the full significance of this because of their inability to comprehend the spirituality of the Catholic faith and the Sacraments of the Church, which accounts for much of the literature depicting scenes and events and containing statements so absurd as to be positively shocking to Catholics. The speaker quoted from some of these publications as an evidence to sustain her argument, and then referred to the "splendid work which Father Zephyrin is doing in writing the histories of these missions," and said—

"Father Zephyrin's Splendid Work deserves the gratitude of every Californian, regardless of creed, for giving us a reliable history of these matchless old missions. Perhaps he was driven to desperation by the amount of drivel that percolates through the public press, pretending to be authentic accounts, and was forced, through a sense of wrong done the noble order of which he is a member, to take up his pen in their defence, but whatever motive prompted the act, history is enriched by the result, and truth is proven, not only stranger, but more fascinating than fiction. Father Englehardt writes from the soul. Every chapter holds the interest of the reader. The pages are fraught with the very atmosphere that surrounded the pioneer padres and attended them in their work of christianizing the Indians, and we have that solid satisfaction while reading these virile lines, of knowing that it is an accurate account of events, compiled from records among the archives of the old missions themselves, and from diaries kept by those pioneer padres, still preserved by their successors in authority. No one should attempt to even touch, ever so lightly, upon this subject without having as a reference and guide this work of Father Englehardt's—*Missions and Missionaries of California.*

"Much of the material secured by Father Englehardt for use in this work was copied from original documents which later were destroyed by the great conflagration in San Francisco following the earthquake of 1906, and therefore would have been utterly lost to history had not a happy inspiration prompted this humble successor of those sturdy pioneer Franciscans to undertake this great task. Future generations will do him honor for having preserved for posterity these invaluable records; but we of the present period should not withhold the credit that is due so great an undertaking, and in every way possible should lend our support and encouragement to the work; for in a very special manner these grand old Missions, with sainted memories clustering round every noble pile, are the heritage of Catholics in California."

From the description presented in the preceding chapter the readers will have learned what was done to save the endangered Mission structures, and by whom the work was accomplished before the close of the memorable year 1911. We therefore continue the narrative of the most important events in Father Buckler's administration, which after the last visit of Bishop Conaty was confined to Santa Inés Valley and to the less distant Los Alamos. Lompoc became an independent parish with a resident priest, and so relieved Father Buckler of that charge, and of its long trips to and from there by slow-going horse and buggy. Sisquoc, about eighteen miles in an opposite direction had been made a station of Santa Maria parish as early as 1907. In consequence, the surviving

INTERIOR OF THE RESTORED MISSION.

Indians and the Mexicans could be given more attention at
Santa Inés. However, they were never neglected. Although
the Father was not able to converse with them in Spanish,
the language they spoke, at Easter time, at least, a Spanish
speaking priest would be invited so that they might have an
opportunity to receive the holy Sacraments.

In April, 1912, it fell to the lot of the writer to conduct
the sacred ceremonies of the last three days of Holy Week,
while the pastor with two students from the Franciscan seminary of Santa Barbara attended to the singing in the organ
loft. It was always strenuous labor, especially as the interior
of the church could not be heated. Easter morning dawned
milder. There were many confessions and likewise on Easter
Monday. We had the satisfaction of knowing that by far
the most if not all the Spanish speaking people availed themselves of their opportunities. Anyway, during the High Mass
on Resurrection Day the church was filled to capacity with
people. Those desirous of receiving holy Communion had
attended the earlier Low Mass at nine o'clock. Others attended to this Annual Duty on the day following.

The solicitous pastor also had the children, Indian as well
as white, learn their Religion from the catechism. For this
purpose he would go to the town of Santa Inés to facilitate
the attendance of the smaller children. The larger girls and
boys came to the church for instructions. In an amusing
letter to the writer the Father gave vent to his satisfaction at
finding the children eager to learn what they must know and
practise. He boasted that they were a match for any of their
size anywhere.

On May 20, 1913, Father Buckler arranged for the celebration of the 30th anniversary of his priesthood. Announcing
the event to the writer, under date of April 30th, the Jubilarian confided to him that "Mamie is making two new dalmatics in white, one more white cope and one veil for Corpus
Christi."

The ever resourceful and practical Miss Goulet later explained as follows: "We found at the Mission a very large

and bulky canopy for processions. It must have been used for out of doors processions, as it was too large and cumbersome to be used in the narrow aisle of the church. I took this large canopy all apart, and out of the silk materials made up two dalmatics, a cope and a benediction veil. I asked Father Nevin of San Miguel Mission for the loan of one of the dalmatics I had seen there so that I could copy the old design. In remodeling or repairing I tried to keep all the vestments in the original designs or styles. I made these up so as to have them ready for use in the celebration."

The Rev. Father inaugurated the jubilee of his ordination in a novel way. First he had the graves of the Franciscan missionaries just outside the sanctuary decorated with flowers. The Solemn High Mass of Requiem for the deceased friars began at 10:30 a. m., Rev. Octavio Villa, S. J., being the celebrant, Rev. J. D. Nevin and Rev. Fr. Zephyrin, O. F. M., assisting as deacon and subdeacon respectively. Instead of a sermon, Fr. Zephyrin read from the Burial Register the entry for each deceased in Spanish, and at the close marked out the grave of each beneath the floor in front of him. A few remarks in English enlightened the assembled people regarding the respective missionary's record as read from the Burial Register. The entries in full will be found in chapter nine of this volume. This memorial service terminated the first part of the day's festivity.

The celebrant and deacons now retired to the sacristy whence the deacons emerged vested in the white dalmatics and the Jubilarian in the white cope made for the occasion as related before. The Rev. C. N. Raley of Lompoc preached the jubilee sermon. This was followed by the Benediction with the Blessed Sacrament. The singing of the "Holy God We Praise Thy Name" by the whole congregation closed the divine services in the church. Thereupon the procession headed by the crossbearer, the Rev. Fr. Aloysius, O. F. M., made its way through the crowded church to the reception room. The photographer, of course, was in evidence as the accompanying engraving bears witness.

The banquet was held in the spacious hall of the museum, or room 18 on the diagram. It was a pleasant affair which need not be reported in detail. It is worthy of note that the ever-neighborly Danes of the adjoining town of Solvang also manifested their appreciation for the genial Jubilarian.

A most important event in the history of Mission Santa Inés was the celebration of the centenary of the Mission church's dedication. This occurred on Independence Day, Wednesday, July 4th, 1917. At ten o'clock in the morning the procession emerged from the front corridor, two young ladies in white bearing the large United States and Papal flags side by side. Next came the crossbearers in surplice, Joseph J. Herlihy and A. A. Koch. Then followed little white and Indian girls dressed in white, the altar boys, the Rev. C. N. Raley of Lompoc as master of ceremonies, and finally the celebrant of the Highmass, Rev. Alexander Buckler, between the deacons Rev. A. Goulet of Santa Barbara and Rev. A. Serra of Montecito. When the clergy had entered the beautifully decorated sanctuary the Highmass began.

After the Holy Mass, celebrant and deacons exchanged the white vestments for the black, and then, standing by the decorated tombs of the deceased Franciscan missionaries, celebrant and deacons sang the "Libera," and at the close the graves were blessed.

Thereupon the procession formed as before and proceeded to the cemetery, where, in front of the great Cross, the "Libera" was repeated, and the graves of all buried in the sacred "God's Acre" were blessed. The procession finally returned to the corridor and disbanded.

Dinner and barbecue was then enjoyed by the hungry multitude.

In the afternoon, on a platform erected in front of the Mission, patriotic and historical addresses were made by Fathers Raley, Serra and Cordeiro, and by Mr. W. J. Ford of Los Angeles, by the Presbyterian Minister of the town of

CELEBRATION OF THE THIRTIETH ANNIVERSARY OF THE PRIESTHOOD OF REV. A BUCKLER.
REV. J. D. NEVIN, DEACON. REV. ZEPHYRIN, O. F. M. SUBDEACON.

Santa Inés, Rev. Dr. Brown, and by the Rev. J. Homesgeld, Lutheran pastor of the Danish settlement of Solvang near the Mission.

Between the speeches lovely Spanish dances were danced by two couples on the same platform.

The exercises closed with singing of the Red, White and Blue, led by Father Buckler himself.

The hardships undergone, together with infirmities at last rendered Father Buckler's duties exceedingly burdensome. Complying with his call for assistance as formerly, April 26-30, 1919, we observed that he had lost much of his vigor and cheerfulness. He was beginning to suffer from umbilical hernia, as we learned some time later. "Nevertheless," Miss Goulet relates, "he performed his duties as well as possible till the year 1922, when the malady became troublesome, and he would complain of constant pain in his side. Winter was approaching, when the cold unheatable rooms added to the discomfort. He longed for more agreeable quarters and a chance to recuperate. Accordingly, the good Father petitioned the Bishop of the Diocese, the Most Rev. John J. Cantwell, D. D., for a leave of six months' absence. It was granted, and the Bishop appointed the Rev. P. A. Quinn temporary pastor. Father Quinn appeared on October 10th, 1922. Father Buckler with his niece in her automobile, purchased some years previously with the generous aid of friends around the country, on Oct. 15, 1922, left for Santa Barbara. Thus it came to pass that Father and I put our little earnings together and bought our home in Santa Barbara."

Father Buckler returned to Santa Inés Mission and resumed charge on April 21, 1923. "I did not return with him," our informant writes, "but as he would have no strange housekeeper, I went back and forth doing all I could. It was very hard for Father to be alone so much of the time, and hard for me to keep up both ends by means of an automobile, and worrying about him when I had to be here.

"This state of things lasted till August 2, 1924, when the

ailing priest received the second leave of absence for three months, which he had desired. The Rev. L. Bourke was sent up to Santa Inés to act as pastor temporarily. Father returned to Santa Barbara.

"As the end of Father's second leave of absence drew near," Miss Goulet relates, "he dreaded more than ever to return to the cold and damp rooms of the Mission for the winter. So rather than go back he on November 2nd, 1924, sent in his resignation to his Bishop."

Bishop Cantwell at once offered Mission Santa Inés to the Provincial of the Franciscans, Very Rev. Fr. Hugolinus Storff. Father Hugolinus declined the offer, whereupon the Bishop offered the Mission to the Capuchin Fathers, who had but recently come from Ireland. Meanwhile the Rev. L. Bourke remained at Santa Inés till the arrival of the Capuchins on November 20th, 1924.

"After a year or so of Santa Barbara climate and a good rest," our faithful informant writes, "Father's health improved and he helped out at the church of Our Lady of Sorrows almost every Sunday until the last two years of his life, when he said the ten-thirty o'clock Mass at Montecito every Sunday. I took him there and back in my car. During the week he would celebrate holy Mass in his own private chapel, a little addition he had built to the house for that purpose.

"However, the pains from the umbilical hernia by November 1929, became acute. He finally called in Dr. Nagelmann. After a consultation with Dr. Burkhard it was decided that an operation was necessary. On November 29th the operation was performed by Dr. Nagelmann assisted by Dr. Burkhard. It was the Father's first experience in a hospital, but he much preferred his home. So to ease matters, I went up every day to wait on him from nine in the morning till eight, nine or ten in the evening. On December 20th, just a month after the operation, I took him home in my car. Though he was still very weak, I had every hope for his recovery. But somehow, when the rains and the weather grew colder, he took to his bed, and grew weaker all the time till the end came on March 7th, 1930. During all this time I nursed him alone day and night, except in the last two weeks when I would not leave him a minute, although I was pretty well worn out. So I asked my sister Emma to come down from San Luis Obispo and help me out. Father's mind was bright and he was conscious to the very last minute. When on March 7th, he motioned with his hand that he wished to be turned to the other side, I put my arm around his neck and shoulders, he looked at me, and I saw the end had come. So poor, dear Father died in my arms, whilst my sister stood by me. We immediately telephoned Father Oyarzo at the parish church, and in five minutes he was with us. Father was well prepared for death. During his illness Father Oyárzo was almost a daily visitor, bringing him holy Communion and annointing him on February 26th. The sick Father was not afraid to die. He gave minute details for the funeral and regarding those to be invited. You know that Father was always very methodical in everything he did, and always trusted me to execute his wishes, which I have done to the smallest particular. He was buried in Calvary Cemetery under the floor of the chapel to the right as you enter.

"The funeral services on March 10th were held in the Mission church of Santa Barbara. At the Requiem Highmass the Rev. Alexander W. Oyárzo, S. J., was the celebrant. Rev. Mathias Ternes, who built the church at Santa Maria, and was for many years a neighbor, served as deacon. The Rev. Ambrose Goulet, a retired priest who for many years would assist Father Buckler during Holy Week, served as subdeacon. The Rev. C. N. Raley, formerly of Lompoc, preached the sermon. When all was over, I had a marble slab with the following inscription placed over the grave:

Rev. Alexander Buckler

Born May 23rd, 1855

Ordained May 19, 1883

Died March 7th, 1930

R. I. P.

"Now Rev. Father, as I said in the beginning, I did not wish to secure any glory for myself; but rather to picture the condition of things at the Mission when Father Buckler and I arrived, and all subsequent events, as well as I could. With that in mind I have tried to relate, as simply as I could the things you wished to know.

Santa Barbara, March 10th, 1932.

Mary Laura Goulet."

APPENDIX

A

SANTA INÉS, VIRGEN Y MARTIR

Saint Agnes, one of the most popular female Saints, was held in the highest esteem through all the ages from the time of her martyrdom about the year 304. St. Jerome, who lived towards the end of the fourth century, declared that the tongues and pens of all nations were employed in glorifying this heroic saint, who conquered both the cruelty of the tyrant and the frailty of her youthful age, and crowned the glory of virginity with that of martyrdom. She had, indeed, always been regarded in the Church as a special patroness of holy purity.

There are no details extant of her family or of her earliest years; but she must have been the daughter of very wealthy parents since the young nobles of Rome eagerly sought Agnes in marriage both for her wealth and her rare beauty. From St. Ambrose and St Augustine we learn that she was not more than thirteen years of age at the time of her glorious death. For all her suitors she had but the one answer: I am already espoused to a heavenly bridegroom, and will have no other. When the young nobles found that nothing could move Agnes to choose any one of them, their esteem for her changed to hatred. In revenge they accused her to the governor of being a Christian.

The judge at first employed the most kindly arguments and made the most tempting promises, but all without effect. She would reply to all he said: I have a heavenly spouse. I will have no other. The judge then ordered a terrible fire started, and had all instruments of torture displayed before the frail maiden. He once more offered her life and liberty if she renounced Christianity, otherwise he would have all the instruments used on her body. Instead of betraying any signs of fear, Agnes expressed her joy at the prospects of suffering for her Beloved Spouse. She was now dragged before some idols and ordered to offer incense to them; but as St. Ambrose relates, Agnes could not be induced to move her hand except for the purpose of making the Sign of the Cross.

Enraged to find himself defeated by a mere girl of thirteen years, the judge threatened to have her sent to a house of wickedness to become the victim of lewd men, if she remained stubborn. To this the holy maiden replied: "You may stain your sword in my blood, but you will never profane my body which is consecrated to Christ, who will protect me." The infuriated judge then commanded her to be taken to the house of wickedness. On the way profligate youths tore all the clothing from her body to have their sport with her. Instantly, however, the hair of her head grew thick and long down to her feet and so covered her person like a mantle. Nevertheless, one of the lecherous men, more bold than the others, attempted to be rude to her. He was instantly stricken with blindness and fell to the ground like one dead.

The governor still more exasperate, then condemned Agnes to be beheaded. Transported with joy on hearing the sentence, she hastened to the place of execution more eagerly than others go to the wedding, as St. Ambrose remarks. On reaching the spot, Agnes knelt for a short prayer, and then bowed her head, which the executioner cut with one stroke of the ax.

The body of the virgin martyr was placed in a tomb on the Via Nomentana, Rome, and around it grew a larger catacomb which bore her name.

During the reign of Constantine, the Great, through the efforts of his daughter Constantia, a basilica was erected over the tomb which contained the remains of the martyr saint. The church was entirely remodeled in the seventh century by Pope Honorius, and it has since remained unaltered.

Since the Middle Ages Saint Agnes by artists has been represented bearing a lamb on her left arm and holding the hilt of a sword in her right hand. At Rome, on her feast, two lambs are solemnly blessed by the Pope, and from the wool *palliums* are made which the Pope sends to newly-appointed Archbishops as a mark of the plenitude of their powers.

B

SPIRITUAL RESULTS—1804 TO 1850—SANTA INES

Year	Baptisms		Marriages		Deaths		M.	F.	Exist.	Confessions	Communions	Confirmations
	Ind.	Wh.	Ind.	Wh.	Ind.	Wh.						
1804...	112	....	18	....	....	....	116	109	225	....	....	....
1805...	....	....	....	....	....	....	....	....	....	....	....	....
1806...	371	4	100	....	118	....	229	341	570	....	....	....
1807...	412	....	116	....	154	....	....	....	587	....	....	....
1808...	445	3	121	1	186	....	272	315	587	26	....	....
1809...	487	....	133	....	210	....	....	....	603	32	1	....
1810...	546	....	146	....	245	....	286	342	628	....	....	....
1811...	591	....	159	....	301	2	280	331	611	215	....	....
1812...	626	1	162	....	338	....	288	323	611	206	....	....
1813...	664	....	178	1	378	1	294	313	607	250	....	....
1814...	695	3	187	....	412	2	277	311	588	285	2	....
1815...	807	2	214	....	473	1	306	330	636	332	18	....
1816...	992	4	278	1	524	....	377	391	768	467	165	....
1817...	1033	....	282	1	609	2	366	354	720	503	264	....
1818...	1063	6	283	....	680	2	353	328	681	541	297	....
1819...	1095	12	299	....	743	1	333	314	647	427	287	....
1820...	1140	....	307	....	789	....	331	304	635	345	237	....
1821...	1170	....	314	....	850	....	318	286	604	393	205	....
1822...	1193	2	329	1	895	2	306	276	582	267	203	....
1823...	1223	....	334	....	944	....	301	263	564	348	279	....
1824...	1235	2	338	1	997	1	254	262	516	....	....	....
1825...	1250	....	353	....	1026	1	245	255	500	240	190	....
1826...	1271	1	359	1	1061	....	234	253	487	200	160	....
1827...	1286	2	370	....	1085	....	233	244	477	210	165	....
1828...	1299	....	385	....	1118	....	....	....	455	203	150	....
1829...	1313	1	386	1	1140	....	218	210	428	....	....	....
1830...	1326	....	389	....	1159	....	....	....	418	....	....	....
1831...	1335	1	390	....	1190	....	205	183	388	80	....	....
1832...	1345	3	400	....	1227	....	196	164	360	....	....	....
1833...	1366	....	407	....	1231	....	....	....	....	....	....	....
1834...	1372	....	410	....	1262	....	....	....	....	....	....	15
1835...	1398	....	420	....	1288	....	....	....	....	....	....	....
1836...	1411	....	422	....	1302	....	....	....	....	....	....	....
1837...	1431	....	429	....	1334	....	....	....	....	....	....	....
1838...	1447	....	437	....	1359	....	....	....	....	....	....	....
1839...	1460	....	442	....	1385	....	....	....	....	....	....	....
1840...	1472	....	446	....	1403	....	....	....	....	....	....	....
1841...	1492	....	450	....	1427	....	....	....	....	....	....	....
1842...	1501	....	453	....	1446	....	....	....	....	....	....	to 159
1843...	1523	....	459	....	1473	....	....	....	....	....	....	....
1844...	1541	....	468	....	1506	....	....	....	....	....	....	to 193
1845...	1558	....	477	....	1528	....	....	....	....	....	....	....
1846...	1574	....	486	....	1546	....	....	....	....	....	....	....
1847...	1586	....	487	....	1573	....	....	....	....	....	....	....
1848...	1608	....	492	....	1600	....	....	....	....	....	....	....
1849...	1622	....	496	....	1620	....	....	....	....	....	....	to 226
1850...	1631	....	497	....	1632	....	....	....	....	....	....	....

MATERIAL RESULTS AT MISSION SANTA INES

AGRICULTURAL PRODUCTS

1804 to 1834

Year	Wheat		Barley		Corn		Beans		Peas		TOTAL		
	Pl.	Hrv.	Pl.	Hrv.	Pl.	Hrv.	Pl.	Hrv.	Pl.	Hrv.	Pl.	Hrv.	Bushels
1804..	36	800	....	.....	2	250	2	22	....	.....	40	1072	1787
1805..	....	.....	....	.....	....	.....	....	.....	....	.....	....	.....	.....
1806..	95	259	....	.....	4	200	2	35	....	.....	101	494	823
1807..	58	157	....	.....	4	380	3	38	1	21	66	596	993
1808..	56	500	4	50	4	500	4	84	1	1	69	1135	1892
1809..	62	700	8	116	5	600	3	70	....	.....	78	1486	2477
1810..	70	1100	20	160	6	1200	4	126	1	66	101	2652	4420
1811..	115	3000	....	.....	6	3000	4	160	3	310	132	6470	10783
1812..	90	3400	....	.....	5	3000	1	80	2	514	98	6994	11657
1813..	47	2000	....	.....	3	1000	3	160	4	520	57	3680	6133
1814..	34	1000	4	60	4	1000	5	200	4	212	61	2472	4120
1815..	100	2000	4	50	4	400	6	90	1	18	115	2558	4263
1816..	60	1200	4	60	3	300	4	160	1	100	72	1820	3033
1817..	140	2500	....	.....	8	2600	4	180	....	.....	152	5280	8600
1818..	150	900	3	200	5	2000	4	140	3	250	165	3490	5817
1819..	90	2000	13	600	2	1000	1	90	3	210	109	3900	6500
1820..	100	900	....	.....	4	1200	4	10	2	166	110	2276	3794
1821..	100	3600	13	800	5	600	6	620	3	319	127	5945	9908
1822..	60	1500	....	.....	5	1000	1	9	....	.....	66	2509	4182
1823..	80	1000	....	.....	6	1000	4	90	1	8	91	2098	3498
1824..	60	600	12	300	3	400	3	12	....	.....	78	1312	2187
1825..	150	2400	11	200	4	800	4	60	1	1	170	3461	5768
1826..	92	1047	....	.....	2	700	6	60	1	8	101	1815	3025
1827..	51	1200	....	.....	2	400	3	70	1	1	57	1671	2785
1828..	57	1200	....	.....	4	140	3	30	....	.....	64	1370	2283
1829..	58	200	....	.....	11	800	4	133	1	23	74	1156	1927
1830..	50	800	....	.....	6	400	4	20	....	.....	60	1220	2033
1831..	106	1282	....	.....	5	300	3	.....	1	.....	115	1582	2637
1832..	50	800	....	.....	6	400	4	20	....	.....	60	1220	2033
1833..	....	.....	....	.....	....	.....	....	.....	....	.....	....	.....	.....
1834..	....	886	....	90	....	100	....	6	....	1	.....	1083	1805

Total Bushels.......................121,163

MATERIAL RESULTS AT MISSION SANTA INES—LIVESTOCK

1804 to 1834

Year	Cattle	Sheep	Goats	Pigs	Mules	Horses	Total
1804........	500	1017	......	......	14	146	1677
1805........	......	......	......	......	......	......	......
1806........	1832	1600	......	......	28	275	3735
1807........	2300	1701	......	......	36	229	4266
1808........	2500	1800	......	......	52	260	4612
1809........	3000	2000	......	......	52	290	5342
1810........	3200	2300	......	......	64	410	5974
1811........	3300	3000	......	60	74	500	6934
1812........	3300	5000	......	200	72	560	9132
1813........	3400	5200	......	300	87	620	9607
1814........	4000	5300	40	200	92	660	10292
1815........	44C0	5600	70	220	94	700	11084
1816........	5000	5000	100	250	116	800	11266
1817........	6000	5000	120	150	120	770	12160
1818........	6000	5500	130	200	126	540	12496
1819........	6000	5500	120	160	130	580	12490
1820........	7000	5000	100	100	120	600	12920
1821........	6000	6000	......	100	120	630	12850
1822........	6500	3500	......	80	124	710	10914
1823........	6000	3000	......	75	114	740	9929
1824........	5800	2400	......	80	100	740	9120
1825........	6000	2800	......	......	110	736	9646
1826........	6400	2700	......	......	120	380	9600
1827........	6500	3600	......	70	130	370	10670
1828........	7000	3000	......	60	100	300	10460
1829........	7100	2800	......	70	100	270	10340
1830........	......	......	......	......	......	......	......
1831........	7300	2200	......	30	112	320	10962
1832........	7200	2100	......	60	110	390	9860
1833........	......	......	......	......	......	......	......
1834........	7000	2000	......	......	60	400	9460

C

FR. BLAS ORDAZ, O. F. M.

"Fr. Blas Ordaz," The Commissary Prefect, Fr. Mariano Payeras, wrote in his Biographical Sketches on December 31, 1820, "is twenty-eight years of age, and his native place is Cervero de Rio Alama, six leagues from Calahora, in the Province of Burgos, Spain. He came to the College of San Fernando de Mexico in 1819, and to this spiritual field of Labor (California) in 1820. Experience will reveal his merits; but he manifests a laudable disposition."

Fr. Ordaz was assigned to Mission Santa Inés from Mission Purisima on March 25, 1824. Since his arrival in California, however, Mexico in 1821 declared itself independent of Spain, and cut off the supply of Franciscan volunteers for the Indian Missions. Fr. Ordaz himself was among the last Fathers who came from the mother country. Worse than that, on March 29, 1829, the Mexican Government decreed that all Spaniards residing in California, New Mexico and other territories should leave the country within one month and the republic within three months after the publication of the law. Although, owing to general protests from settlers, the decree was not executed in California, by the year 1830 nearly all the Missions had each but one Franciscan Father to look after the spiritual and temporal needs of the neophytes. Fr. Narciso Durán himself at Mission San José stood alone, and therefore could not make the canonical visitations as was the custom before. In fact no visitations took place since 1821. This was due to the animosity of Governor Echeandia who prevented Fr. Commissary Prefect Sarria from exercising his duty by declaring him under arrest. Fr. Durán on becoming Presidente could find no substitute to take charge of his Mission even temporarily.

If under favorable conditions, when two Fathers sustained each other, regular visitations were regarded as indispensable for preserving religious discipline and religious fervor, the periodical visits of the Fr. Presidente became imperative when the individual missionary labored alone.

The Missionaries, in their Religion, in the Sacraments, and in the Rules of their Order, possessed abundant consolations and powerful incentives for the conscientious performance of their duties. Without them they could not have weathered the never-ending tempest of opposition, oppression, privations and all sorts of disheartening difficulties. Then the utter loneliness!—This caused Fr. Presidente Lasuén to call the lonely missionary's existence in California "a life without consolation, an infirmity without aid, and a death without Sacraments."—Again he wrote: "I oppose and resist the project of living alone at a Mission."—Furthermore he declared: "No one can convince me that I must subject myself to such a solitude in this ministry." It was against their Rules, against Papal

Regulations,[1] and against the Spanish laws for Religious. The periodical presence of the solicitous and sympathetic Superior would have the effect of correcting what might be faulty, of removing temptations, reviving zeal, clearing away doubts, and cheering the missionaries generally. This boon of security in their ministry was lacking from 1821 to 1833. Only one visit of a fellow missionary occurred at Santa Inés from 1824 to 1833, and this was the appearance of Fr. Juan Moreno, who February 11, 1829, administered Baptism there.

The neophyte population of Mission Santa Inés ranged between 516 in 1824 to 360 at the end of 1832. For them Fr. Blas Ordaz had to supply the temporal as well as spiritual needs. It does not appear that he neglected his duties in any line, although he did the work of two men. He reported in detail annually as prescribed, and contracted no debts which might embarrass a successor.

Not having any one to transact Mission business with merchants and skippers at the port of Santa Barbara, Fr. Ordaz, accompanied by a guard or an Indian, would on horseback make the journey by way of Las Cruces and Rancho del Refugio, and attend to the exchange of goods himself. This we infer from the Mission circumstances as revealed in the early chapters and reports. He would have gone there oftener for the Sacrament of Penance, too. On his way back and forth he would stop at the Refugio Rancho of the Ortega family for meals and to feed his horse. Nothing unfavorable was ever said of the good Father until the year 1832, according to Fernandito, who had the story from the Indians when more than twenty years later he settled down among the neophytes of Santa Inés Mission.

It was claimed that Fr. Ordaz had purchased a new carpet for the church at Santa Inés, and then had given away the old carpet to a widow with two children who belonged to the Ortega family at Refugio. This action angered the Indians, because they regarded everything about the church as belonging to the Indians, and that Fr. Ordaz therefore, had done wrong to give the carpet away to an outsider. He may, like Fr. Uria before him, have incurred their displeasure for something else which they failed to reveal. They went further in keeping with their jealous and carnal nature, they let their imagination run riot and accused the Father of wrong dealings with the woman whom they called Poyorena (Pollorena), presumably the name of her deceased husband. That is all Fernandito could tell us.

We now proceed to examine the official reports for the purpose of ascertaining just what was purchased in 1832, and given away, if the Indians told the truth. Accordingly we find that on December 31, 1832, Fr. Ordaz under the head *Iglesia*, reports: "Se ha añadido dos comodas y *un juego de alfombras* para el adorno de la *sacristia*."—"There have been

---

[1] See Appendix **F** for *Apostolic Colleges* in *The Missions and Missionaries*, volume I.

added two chests with drawers, and one set of carpet rugs for the adorning of the sacristy." Hence, the jealous Indians had things somewhat mixed. This probably occurred in the summer when ships would land at Santa Barbara to trade goods for Mission produce.

The clique of jealous Indians went still further, and resolved to send a delegation from among themselves to Monterey, in order to inform Fr. Presidente Narciso Durán, so Fernandito relates; but Fr. Durán was stationed at Mission San José, much farther north. They probably met Fr. Ex-Comisario Prefecto Vicente de Sarria, who would have questioned them and told them that he would report their complaints to Fr. Durán. At all events, under date of September 18, 1832, Fr. Durán issued a Circular in Latin which was to make the rounds of the Missions from Santa Clara to San Diego, to be transcribed in the *Libro de Patentes* of every local Mission, signed by the resident missionary, and returned to himself at San José Mission. The document is quite long. It would cover six typewritten pages. Therein the Fr. Presidente warns the friars everywhere to live worthy of their calling, not to give scandal in any way, to avoid unnecessary communication with the other sex, in short to edify and not to disedify. He furthermore uses very strong language concerning some friar, whom he does not name, who was not conducting himself in accordance with the priestly dignity and the Rules of St. Francis.

The Fathers everywhere, most of whom had grown old and infirm in the Missions, may have wondered why the Fr. Presidente had not addressed the culprit directly, and him alone. They needed sympathy and encouragement, for already dark clouds were gathering and threatening the destruction of the Missions. Fr. Durán had made an unwise move, to say the least, not at all in harmony with the directions laid down by St.Francis, in thus prejudging one of the missionaries on the testimony of disgruntled Indians; whereas it was the rule in the civil as well as in the ecclesiastical tribunals of Mexico and South America never in serious cases to admit the testimony of Indians unless it was supported by at least two unimpeachable witnesses. (See our *Missions and Missionaries*, volume first, Appendix **H**, on *Indian Veracity*.) At any rate, Fr. Ordaz was entitled to a hearing before action was taken on the complaints of the Indians. Fr. Durán would most probably never have issued the Circular lecturing the missionaries on general principles, if he had previously allowed Fr. Ordaz to explain his action or conduct. The Fr. Presidente, who quotes Holy Scripture, might well have considered St. Paul to the *Colossians*, iii, 21. Evidently Fr. Narciso Durán was not the fatherly Presidente Fr. Junípero Serra was. The Indians thereafter had no more complaints to make.

Fr. Ordaz, very much embittered, for the time being nursed his grievance in silence, but not in Christian resignation as the sequel shows. Early in 1833, ten Mexican Franciscans arrived in California and took charge of the northern Missions. This allowed the Fernandinos or Spanish Franciscans to withdraw and make necessary changes. Thus in May Fr.

Ordaz was transferred to Mission San Buenaventura, Fr. José Joaquin Jimeno taking his place at Santa Inés. Fr. Presidente Durán himself moved to Santa Barbara.

On reaching Mission San Buenaventura, his pent-up anger exploded to the extent that he would endeavor to annoy Fr. Durán, his superior, when there was a chance, especially by joining politicians and other worldly people to divert himself on visiting Santa Barbara town. This went on for about two years unknown to the public, save that Fr. Durán made Governor Figueroa a confidant of the facts, in consequence of which Fr. Ordaz recovered his moorings, and a great calm ensued. Thereafter he made an excellent record for himself at Mission San Fernando and later at Mission San Gabriel where he died much respected on November 11, 1850, the last of the Spanish Franciscans. (See for details *The Missions and Missionaries*, vol. iii, pp. 572-576.)

However, all this does not concern us at Santa Inés. What affects us here is the following assertion of Bancroft: "Padre Blas was a lively and good natured man, but his fondness for women involved him occasionally in scandal and reprimand from his Superiors." (*Calfornia*, vol. iv, page 759.)

We have examined every page indicated by Bancroft in his *Biographical Sketches* as containing references to Fr. Blas Ordaz; but we have not discovered so much as an allusion which would justify the unscrupulous prevaricator's clause on "fondness for women." It is just thrown in, as it were, to make his statement sound piquant. That is nothing new with him. In several of our histories we have had to expose Bancroft's fondness for besmirching the reputation of priests and Religious. On that subject he stands on a level with disgruntled Indians, and is just as reliable.

From his personal accountbook, discovered but lately in the Santa Barbara Mission Archives, we learn that the kindhearted Fr. Blas Ordaz allowed the settlers and laborers in the Santa Inés region to purchase foodstuffs, dressgoods, blankets and shoes at the Mission warehouse. The weaving rooms produced various kinds of cloth, and the Indian shoe makers furnished footwear to suit. Cereals, vegetables and fruits were raised in the Mission fields, gardens and orchards. Fleshmeat could be had fresh right on the spot, and tallow candles were in stock. This arrangement afforded great relief to the people who otherwise were compelled to obtain such goods from distant Santa Barbara, when roads were but trails and the slow oxcart the only vehicle. On the other hand, it must have been a most distracting burden for the priest, who single-handed at the same time had to provide for his neophyte family of nearly four hundred men, women and children.

Incidentally we become aware of the fact that even at this early date, less than thirty years after the founding of the Mission, the white population had grown quite numerous, as we may infer from the list of customers named in Fr. Ordaz's accountbook.

The list of names begins with Mathias Cordero on January 18, 1829. Then follow Albino Zurita, Carlos Lorenzana, Francisco Quijada, Rafael Piño, José Antonio Ortega, José Antonio Valenzuela, Petra Varela, Juan Cordero, Miguel Cordero, Francisco Avila, José Ignacio Lugo, Martin Ruiz, Trinídad Lugo, Antonio Lários, Lazaro Piño, Carmen Dominguez, José Arellanes, Maria Arellanes, Joaquin Villa, Miguel Pico, Vicente Pico, Ramon Valdez, Martin Ortega, Pablo Venegas, Fernando Tico, Daria Ortega, Rafael Gonzalez, and George Allen, a Scotch-Irishman, who on January 27, 1833, began to serve the Mission (entró a servir a esta Mision) for eight pesos a month, three almudes of corn, one almud of beans, three pounds of tobacco, one-half pound of manteca, one-quarter of beef a week, and ten pesos worth of soap a year. He settled up with Fr. Ordaz on May 5, 1833, the last transaction of Father Blas in behalf of Mission Santa Inés.

Finally we become acquainted with the mayordomos of Mission Santa Inés at this period. The first one was José Antonio Valenzuela, who entered upon his duties as mayordomo on June 2, 1829, at the rate of six pesos a month, three almudes of corn, half an almud of beans, four pounds of manteca a week, two reáles worth of soap a month and a candle a day.

Another mayordomo was José Antonio Domingues, who began serving on May 5, 1830, for ten pesos a month besides a quarter of beef, five almudes of corn, one almud of beans, four pounds of manteca, and one peso's worth of soap a week, and a candle a day.

The third mentioned was Joaquin Villa, who begins to serve as mayordomo on December 1st, 1830, at eleven pesos a month, twelve reáles of soap and six cattle a year, five almudes of corn and five pounds of manteca a week, and daily one candle.

D

RANCHERIAS OF MISSION SANTA INES

(According to the Baptismal Register)

Alajulapu (Santa Inés Mission Site.)

Achi or La Quemada

Aguama or Ahuam

Ahuamhone

Alacupusque

Anajue or Najue

Aquep

Aquitchumu

Aseguil

Asil or Casil

Calahuasa

Cuyama or Cuiam

Esjaliuilimu

Eslait

Gelihahuinat

Gerepi

Gualpa

Guaslaique

Guasliac

Guisapa

Haequep, Jequeps, Gequep

Ichaumeu

Jalihuilimu

Jonjonata or Jonata

Matilja

Nomgio

Quitsum

Sactapaquiahua

Sajuchu

Suchi or La Quemada

Segene or Sgene

Sihuecon

Sisahuc

Sisuchu

Sisolop

Sisahuo

Sihuicomo or Zinycon

Sonsococ

Sotonocmu

Stucu or Stuco

Susmulahuit

Names from the Islands.

Cheaumeu

Choluchuch

Cholisus

Cilimi

Elehuachcuyu

Gemascuy

Guililic

Ichaumeu

Jelcuascues

Jeleaicui

Lacayamu or Lacayam

Nimgelgel

Niacla

Nilalui

Silimet

Siucsin

(All from Limú)

DIOS TE SALVE MARIA

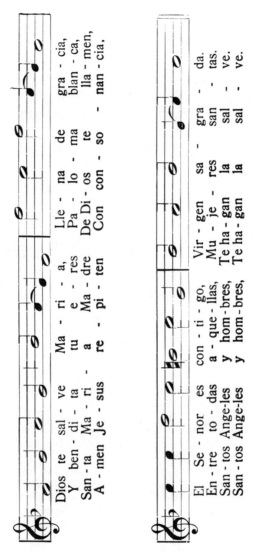

Dios te sal - ve Ma - ri - a, Lle - na de gra - cia,
Y ben - di - ta tu e - res Pa - lo - ma blan - ca,
San - ta Ma - ri - a Ma - dre De Di - os te lla - men,
A - men Je - sus re - pi - ten Con con - so - nan - cia.

El Se - nor es con - ti - go, Vir - gen sa - gra - da
En - tre to - das a - que - llas, Mu - je - res san - tas.
San - tos Ange-les y hom-bres, Te ha - gan la sal - ve.
San - tos Ange-les y hom-bres, Te ha - gan la sal - ve.

E

SINGING AT DIVINE SERVICES AT MISSION
SANTA INÉS

The singers were men who had been chosen in their boyhood, and carefully trained for their good voices. Of course they were taught reading and writing.

They would sing the Gregorian Chant in the choir loft or gallery in the rear of the church. Access to it was through the little room on the ground floor next to the church facing the inner court or patio. From there the stairs led to the loft or gallery. During the few years when the seminary existed at the Mission, 1844-1850, the seminarians recited the Divine Office with the Fathers in this gallery.

The Indian singers would sing the *Introitus* and all other portions of the High Mass as found in the Graduale or large music sheets and books having the parts in square notes. Vespers also were sung from the Vesperale. Even much later, when but few of the singers survived, whenever there would be a High Mass the Gregorian or Plain Chant was sung, as we know from Miss Donohue's narrative.

Instrumental music was played by the band, not as accompaniment, but when the singing terminated in places. Violin, violoncello, baseviolo, and even a triangle constituted the musical outfit.

The chief singers at Mission Santa Inés were Luis Anasoyu as bass, and Venancio Lamlawinat as contralto.

During Holy Week all the singing and the ceremonies were observed. The *Mandatum*, during which the officiating priest would in the sanctuary wash the feet of some old Indian men, was carried out musically by the Indian choir. A violin would indicate the right tone or note. Everything was practised with the missionary beforehand.

The first Indians of the Mission were such as had belonged to Mission Santa Barbara, but were natives of the Santa Inés district. When the Mission was started, those who wished could leave Santa Barbara Mission and join Santa Inés. It was a great help to the Fathers, because these neophytes would introduce the customs they had learned at the older Mission. In matters musical they followed the older Mission choir. They were especially enthusiastic about Father Lasuén, the Superior of all the Missions, who would stay at Santa Barbara at times. He must have been a great musician in church music, for the neophytes at Santa Inés many years later would again mention "Dehunto Padre Lashuen" (Defunto Padre Lasuén) as authority on anything concerning their singing.

On great feasts, and also on Sundays, the Rosary would be recited in the evening. The choir would sing in Spanish or Latin the *Pater Noster*, *Ave Maria*, the *Gloria Patri* and the Mystery, whereupon the missionary or

YA VIENE EL ALBA

1. Ya vie - ne el al - ba rom - pien do el di - - a,
2. Na - cio Ma - ri - a pa - ra con - sue - lo
3. Na - cio Ma - ri - a con e - ra ca - - cia,
4. La sier - pe fie - ra llo - ra sus pe - nas,
5. El in - dos er - no tres ve - ces tiem - bla,
6. To - dos can - te - mos en al - ta la voz,

Di - ga - mos to - dos: A - ve luz Ma - ri - a.
De pe - ca - do - res y luz del cie - lo.
A - ve Ma - ri - a, lle - na de gra - cia.
Mari - a de pon - to, fuer - tes ca - de - nas.
Al de - cir Ma - ri - a, A - ve Ma - ri - a.
A - ve Ma - ri - a, Ma - dre de Di - os.

later the secular priests would recite in Spanish the Hail Mary ten times with the people. A litany would also be recited, or sung.

The *Viene El Alba* would be sung after the prayers at daybreak, as the name implies—*The Dawn is coming*.

The alcalde would go around the village and call out: *A misa! A Misa!* In this way also other services were announced.

"Thus the Indians during the Mission period," Fernandito wistfully related, "had happy times. It was a pity they were not allowed to continue to live in that manner always." They had to yield to white greed. Satan himself must have envied the neophytes.

Fernandito himself loved to sing with the Indians in their homes or in their camps the old Spanish songs which the missionary Fathers had introduced. He wrote a number of them out for us. We reproduce the titles of them. Foremost, here as everywhere, the *ALABADO*, or *Song of PRAISES*, with 24 verses was the most notable. The other hymns were, *DIOS TE SALVE, MARIA.—SALVE GUADALUPE—ALABARIZA DE MARIA SANTISIMA—SALVE MARIA, LUNA HERMOSA—SALVE, MAR DE PENAS*, to the Sorrowful Mother.—*AL DIVINO PESCADOR.—PASION DE NUESTRO SEÑOR JESUS CRISTO.—AL GLORIOSO SAN JOSÉ.—A SAN FRANCISCO DE ASIS.—AL GLORIOSO SAN ANTONIO.—*

F

FERNANDITO

Fernando Cardenas, for his short stature called Fernandito, was born at San José, Peru, as the son of Rafael Cardenas, native of Ecuador, and Tomasa Arrarte, native of Mission Colan, nine miles from the seaport of Paita, Peru. When thirteen years old, he came to California in 1850, in the company of Captain José Yndart and family. The captain had agreed to return the boy to Peru after eight months; but he died on a voyage and was buried at sea. Fernandito seems to have found himself in good hands, and therefore remained in the country. After living for sometime in Los Angeles and San Francisco, he settled down among the Indians near Mission Santa Inés, which thereafter he considered his home. Even at the age of eighty-one his mind was clear and strong. He could remember events of the past, to which he had been an eyewitness, with accuracy, and spoke of them in an interesting manner.

Living so near, he would make himself useful at the Mission and its religious services. He would lead in the public prayers and at singing, and thus became a great factor in the preservation of the Faith and the religious customs of the surviving Indians, since he was well informed on Church matters and loved his Religion dearly. In civil affairs he was also well informed and scrupulously honest, so that the Government Officials at Washington trusted him implicitly, as numerous letters in the possession of the writer demonstrate.

We ourselves consulted him frequently, and were thus enabled to state many important occurences of the past correctly.

Fernandito was never married. Once, indeed, a Mexican girl agreed to marry him. When all was in readiness, and before the banns were finally published, he gave the girl fifty dollars to obtain an outfit for herself at Santa Barbara. She took the fifty dollars, but married another man. Fernandito was not heartbroken at all. On the contrary, he took the matter philosophically and declared with great good humor that it was worth fifty dollars to get rid of her.

Miss Mary Goulet, who kindly supplied these and the following items, relates that "five or six years before Fernandito's death, when the old, little man was beginning to weaken, Father Buckler offered him a room at the Mission. He declined and said that he wanted to be a free man, which probably meant that he did not wish to be under obligations to any one. Then Father gave him the use of three acres of Mission land, just in front of the Mission, but below the bluff He also let him have the lumber left over from the restoration work, to build for himself a little house of two rooms. Some of Fr. Bucklers friends also gave him twenty-five dollars with which he bought a bed and a cookstove besides other things he needed. He then raised vegetables for our use at the Mission, besides tamale corn and chili, tomatoes and cantaloupes which he sold. He also saved the corn husks which he took to Santa Barbara in the fall and sold to tamale parlors or wherever they were used.

In time he grew more and more feeble and, at the age of eighty years, he found it difficult to live and work in this way. Father Buckler then secured for him the county aid. Thereupon the good old creature would more often be seen at Santa Barbara. Not having any relatives, he would stop at what was called the Borderre or French Hotel in the City Hall Plaza with his friends the Borderre family.

"The last time he came from Santa Inés Mission was about the end of January, 1919. It was for the purpose of attending the funeral of a Mexican woman who had passed away, and for whom, as was customary, he lead in reciting the Rosary in Spanish for the deceased woman. He little thought that his own funeral would occur very soon. It was during the epidemic of the Grippe or Influenza. Later in the evening he returned to the Borderre hotel and stayed there till he died on February 7th, just a week to the day that he had led in the prayers for the Mexican woman. It would seem that the Grippe had seized him also. On February 6th he complained of not feeling very well, and then retired early. Mr. Borderre, who was at that time still living, brought him a hot drink, and later went into the room and found Fernandito sound asleep.

1. FERNANDITO WITH REV. A. BUCKLER.
2. REPAIRING RUINED PORTION OF MISSION. REV. A. BUCKLER ON LADDER.
3. FERNANDO CARDENAS (FERNANDITO.)
4. NORTH END OF MISSION QUADRANGLE.

"Next morning the chambermaid found him dead in bed. Mr. Borderre said that he lay in the same position as he had left him the night before. Fernandito had quietly passed away without a struggle. On account of the epidemic of Influenza the body was not taken to the parish church; but one of the Jesuit Fathers went out to the cemetery, recited the usual prayers and blessed the grave in the large vault or mortuary, in the upper row, to the right as you enter, grave number 21. On the marble slab that seals the grave is this inscription:

Fernandito Cardenas

Died February 7th, 1919

R. I. P.

"Mrs. Borderre repeated what Fernandito had told me," Miss Mary Goulet tells us, "about having a lot and house in Santa Barbara which he was leaving to defray his funeral expenses. This was sold by the attorney, who had been entrusted with the transaction, for three hundred dollars. Mrs. Borderre furthermore related that the funeral expenses amounted to five hundred dollars, and that his friends had made up the deficiency. They had also had a Requiem Mass celebrated for the repose of his soul, and later still other holy Masses were ordered for him, because they all had been very fond of him."

G

THE NEOPHYTE INDIAN VILLAGE

According to Fernandito, the Indian Mission village was built of adobes. The walls were whitewashed within and without. The roof was a gable roof and covered with tiles. The group of buildings measured from east to west two hundred feet; from north to south, two hundred and sixty-four feet. Four streets, thirty-one feet wide ran from east to west, and divided the group into three double rows of one story structures about thirty-one feet wide, and a single row of rooms on either end of the group. These two rows of single rooms measured fifteen and one-half feet in width each; the outside walls were two feet thick.

The rooms were partitioned off from one another by an adobe wall of about a foot in thickness. Thus in one row there would be twelve rooms measuring about 15 feet square. There would then twelve Indian families occupy the twelve rooms of a row. Only the children under twelve years of age would remain with parents. Each room had a door and a window on the side to the street. In the walls, cupboards and shelves were provided for the use of the family. The furniture would consist of a bed and another for the children, a table and benches. Hence they had sufficient room for all needs.

The population of the neophyte village would consist of about 450 souls, or 120 families.

Marriageable girls, and single women, besides young widows had their apartments in the spacious loft of the southern end of the front wing in the Mission, where they passed the night unmolested. During the daytime they were occupied in the shops and rooms on the ground floor. When they finished their tasks the girls could visit their relatives in the village close by.

Single men and grown up boys had their quarters near the pozolero or general kitchen.

In 1855 the Indians were forced to vacate the village, and therefore moved to what became known as Zanja Cota Reservation. Only Coleta, and old Indian woman, 90 years of age, refused to leave, and was accordingly allowed to remain till she died.

During the revolt of 1824 a number of Indian rebels, young men, retreated to the last double row in the village which lay between the two last streets, and barricaded themselves against the soldiers. To force them out, the soldiers threw firebrands to the doors and windows. The heat and smoke then compelled the rebels to surrender. The row of buildings which they had occupied was destroyed by the fire and never rebuilt.

H

THE MISSION BELFRY AT SANTA INÉS MISSION
AND ITS BELLS

In Chapter Three, of this volume, mention is made of a belfry adjoining the church edifice. We saw and examined the bells for the first time in 1904. George Wharton James, the noted author, two years later viewed the bells and wrote about them as follows in his *In And Out Of The Old Missions*, page 265: "There are five bells at Santa Inés, and I was interested enough to obtain their pitch. There are two D's and three F's, in two octaves.

"The inscription on one of the bells bears the legend: "Manuel Vargas me fecit ano 1818." (Manuel Vargas made me in 1818.) Another: "Ave Maria Purisima 1807." The one to the right is inscribed: "S. S. (Señor San) Juan Bautista ano de 1803." Still another: "Me fecit ano de 1818, Lima, Mision de la Purisima de la Nueba California." There is no inscription on the top bell, but this top bell has an interesting wooden frame holding it, by means of which it was intended it should be swung."

Bells played an important part in the life of the Christianized Indian. They would announce his birth as well as his death, although in different tones so that all, even at a distance, understood. The drowsy or inattentive worshipper would be reminded of the coming of the Lord at the Consecration in holy Mass, or at Benediction, by the vigorous tones of the little bell or chimes in the hands of the alert altar boy. Then for the various portions of every day, for worship, work, or rest, the bells had their say. The Indian neophyte, indeed, could not imagine a joyful festivity without the tuneful voice of the bell in the church belfry.

Processions were frequent. As the whole community would take part, reciting the Rosary, and singing the delightful Spanish hymns, bells would accompany all with their own cheering sound which gripped the very heart strings of the happy participants. The principal processions during the year were prescribed for the open air as early as February 7, 1775, by the Missionary College of San Fernando de Mexico. They were as follows: Candlemas Day, Palm Sunday, the Rogation Days, and the grand Corpus Christi Day. Besides these, processions were held on other occasions, such as Rosary Sunday and during the Month of May. Throughout these solemnities the Mission bells were in strong evidence and enhanced the celebrations decidedly. In truth, without the joyous peals of the tower bells, to the Indians, and to others as well, all processions would appear veritable funeral marches, which left no room for triumphant rejoicings, such as Mother Church manifests the world over, notably, on Corpus Christi Day, the feast of the Triumph of the Holy Eucharist.

Indeed, church bells were deemed so indispensable for the success of Mission activities and for the good cheer of the neophyte life that, invariably, and at the expense of the Pious Fund, two bells of about a hundredweight were sent to California along with the church goods on founding a Mission.

I

THE CAPUCHIN FRANCISCANS

"The beginnings of the Capuchin Reform are vested with romance and adventure. No one man can be said to be its creator," writes Father Cuthbert, himself a Capuchin, in *The Eccelesiastical Review*, February, 1928.

Nevertheless, we know from the same writer that a Fr. Matteo de Bassi of the Diocese of Fermo, Italy, in 1525, just three hundred years after the death of St. Francis of Assisi, became desirous of living more strictly in accordance with the Rule of St. Francis, especially with regard to poverty than he found it practiced among the Franciscans, better known as *Friars Minor of the Observance* since the reform instituted by St. Bernardine of Sienna a century before. He accordingly went to Rome for the purpose of obtaining the permit to lead the life of a hermit so as to observe strict poverty as prescribed by St. Francis. He also asked permission to wear the hood sewed on the habit after the Camaldolese hermits of that period. Both petitions were granted by Pope Clement VII. Fr. Matteo also adopted the custom of wearing a flowing beard like the monks in their hermitages.

On his return to Fermo, several other friars from the ranks of the Observants joined him. Many others subsequently seceded from the Franciscans with the result that Pope Clement VII on July 3, 1528, by the Bull "Religionis Zelus" released Fr. Matteo and his companions from their obedience to the Observants, and constituted them a distinct religious organization. In the Papal Brief of January 12, 1535, moreover, Pope Paul III applied to them a distinct name—*Capucini*-Capuchins, which has clung to them ever since.

Thereafter the new Order grew rapidly, so that at the chapter of 1537 the members counted 500 friars which number was swelled to 6000 in 1587. At the time of Pope Urban VIII, year 1643, the membership was over 17,000 in forty-two provinces. At the general chapter of 1754, there were represented sixty-three provinces which numbered 32,000 friars. During the political disturbances on the European continent the Capuchins suffered severe losses like all religious Orders. During the latter part of the nineteenth century, however, a revival set in, so that in 1889 the Order of Capuchins in 636 communities consisted of 7852 friars.

At the present time, according to Official Reports, the Capuchin Order the world over has in 56 Provinces 11,249 members. Two of these Provinces with 423 Fathers and Brothers operate in the United States. In addition, there are 33 Fathers and 7 Brothers, subject to the Provincial in Ireland, laboring in parishes of California and Pennsylvania. Furthermore, 18 Fathers, 6 clerics and 2 Brothers constitute the Italian-American Commissariat.

INDEX

A

Abella, Fr. Ramon, O. F. M., 107, 113, 114, 115

Agnes, St., Virgin and Martyr, 10, 174

Aguichumú, Cañada of, 5

Ahuama, Rancheria of, 10

Ahuaslayec, Rancheria of, 4

Alajulapu, Rancheria of, 3, 7, 8, 84

Alaman, Don Lucas, 30

Alcaldes, Indian, 100

Alemany, Most Rev. José Sadoc, O. P., 73, 75, 76, 81, 82, 93, 97, 100, 101, 102

Alisal, Cañon, 120

Alisguey, Cañada of, 54

Aloya, Indian Captain, 88

Aloysius, Fr. O. F. M., 167

Alvarado, J. B. Governor, 46, 47, 48, 57

Amat, Most Rev. Thaddeus, C. M., 93, 100

Ambrís, Doroteo, Subdeacon, 55

Amestoy, Fr. Marcos, O. F. M., 117

Anajue, Rancheria of, 4

Annual Report, 90

Apparel, Wearing, 21

Aquila Joaquin, 67

Aquitsumu, Rancheria of, 4

Argüello, Governor, 35

Arrillaga, José Joaquin de, 4, 6, 8, 11, 87

Arroyo Grande, 139

Asnisehuc, Rancheria of, 4

Atsililihu, Rancheria of, 7

Auto-de-Visíta, 89

Avila, José de los Santos, 55

B

Bacca, Rev. Miguel, 119

Bachelot, Very Rev. J. A. Alejo, 110

Bancroft, 32, 37, 38, 46, 66, 68, 89, 182

Basso, Rev., 104, 119, 120, 121, 122

Beale, E. F., Surveyor General, 81

Bell Tower, Importance of, 192; Restoration of, 149

Bernard, Franciscan Brother, 101

Biddy, Fr. Albert, O. M. Cap., 119

Biennial Report, 116

Bigraphical Sketches, 110

Borderre, (French) Hotel, 189; Family, 189; Mrs., Testimony of, 191

Borica, Diego, Governor, 4

Boussier, Rev. Theodosius, C. SS. CC., 70, 72, 88, 94, 97, 119

Bot, Joaquin, Rev., 119

Bourke, Rev. L., 119, 171

Brown, Rev. Dr., Presbyterian Minister, 170

Buckler, Rev. Alexander, 117, 119, 131, 132, 134, 136, 138, 140, 143, 146, 152, 160, 164, 166, 168, 170, 172, 173, 189

Building Activities, 22, 29, 36

Burial Register, 90; Title Page, 90; First Entry, 90

Burkhard, Dr. Adrian, 171

Buttler, Fr. Casimir, O. M. Cap., 119

C

Cabot, Fr. Pedro, O. F. M., 110

Cabrera, Alejo Salmon Agapito, 55

Calabaza, Cañada of, 54

Calahuasa, Rancheria of, 3, 4, 6, 8, 10

LAUS DEO

Distance from Mission Santa Barbara—12 leagues.
Distance from Mission Purisima— 8 leagues.

The Missions of California

(Correct dates of their founding)

San Diego de Alcala, July 16, 1769.

San Carlos Borromeo, or Carmelo, June 3, 1770.

San Antonio de Padua, July 14, 1771.

San Gabriel, Arcangel, September 8, 1771.

San Luis Obispo, September 1, 1772.

San Francisco de Asis, or Dolores, June 29, 1776.

San Juan Capistrano, November 1, 1776.

Santa Clara de Asis, January 12, 1777.

San Buenaventura, March 31, 1782.

Santa Barbara, December 4, 1786.

La Purisima Concepcion, December2, 1787.

Santa Cruz, August 28, 1791.

La Soledad, October 9, 1791.

San José, June 11, 1797.

San Juan Bautista, June 24, 1797.

San Miguel, Arcangel, July 25, 1797.

San Fernando Rey, September 8, 1797.

San Luis Rey, June 13, 1798.

Santa Inés, September 17, 1804.

San Rafael, Arcangel, December 14, 1817.

San Francisco Solano, July 4, 1823.

FATHER ENGELHARDT'S
HISTORICAL WORKS

ILLUSTRATED

The Franciscans in California. Edition Exhausted.

The Franciscans in Arizona. Edition Exhausted.

The Holy Man of Santa Clara. Edition Exhausted.

Vida del P. Magín Catalá, O. F. M., Spanish. Cloth $1.00

The Missions and Missionaries of California, Vol. I. Eecond Edition, 810 pages. Bound in cloth $4.00

The Missions and Missionaries of California. Vol. II. Second Edition, Cloth. 730 pages $4.00

The Missions and Missionaries of California. Vol. III. Cloth. 680 pages $4.00

The Missions and Missionaries of California. Vol. IV. Cloth. 832 pages $4.00

Index for volumes ii-iv. Cloth. 190 pages $1.50

Above set of five books by mail or express $15.00

Mission San Diego. The Mother of the Missions. Cloth. 372 pages..$2.50

Mission San Luis Rey. The King of the Missions. Cloth. 275 pages..$2.00

Mission San Juan Capistrano. The Jewel of the Missions. Cloth 270 pages $2.00

Mission San Gabriel. The Pride of the Missions. Cloth. 370 pages..$2.00

Mission San Fernando. The Mission of the Valley. Cloth. 170 pages $1.50

Mission Santa Barbara. The Queen of the Missions. Cloth. 488 pages $3.00

Mission San Francisco, or Mission Dolores. Cloth. 450 pages........$2.50

Mission San Miguel, Mission San Antonio, Mission Soledad, the three in one volume. Cloth. 350 pages..........................$2.50

Mission San Buenaventura. The Mission by the Sea. Cloth...........$1.75

Mission San Juan Bautista, A School of Church Music...... ....$1.50